Maui island Travel and Tourism

Vacation, Holiday, Environmental Information

Author
Charles Pearce

Copyright Notice

Copyright © 2017 Global Print Digital
All Rights Reserved

<u>Digital Management Copyright Notice</u>. This Title is not in public domain, it is copyrighted to the original author, and being published by **Global Print Digital**. No other means of reproducing this title is accepted, and none of its content is editable, neither right to commercialize it is accepted, except with the consent of the author or authorized distributor. You must purchase this Title from a vendor who's right is given to sell it, other sources of purchase are not accepted, and accountable for an action against. We are happy that you understood, and being guided by these terms as you proceed. Thank you

First Printing: 2017.

ISBN: 978-1-912483-08-2

Publisher: Global Print Digital.
Arlington Row, Bibury, Cirencester GL7 5ND
Gloucester
United Kingdom.
Website: www.homeworkoffer.com

Table of Content

Touristic Introduction... 1
History 13
    Maui Arts & Culture... 25
    Atmosphere 26
    Festivals of Maui 33
Travel and Tourism... 36
    Maui Travel Tips 37
    Maui Ecotourism 41
    Maui Adventures 43
    Weather 43
    Your First Trip to Maui... 44
    Having Fun 45
        Family Fun on Maui 46
        Haleakala National Park Maui 47
        Pools of Oheo 48
        Hana Maui 50
        Kihei 51
        Maui Honeymoons 52
        Beaches.. 53
            Makena Beach State Park (Big Beach) 54
            Kaanapali Beach.. 55
            West Maui Beaches 56
            East Maui Beaches 57
        Maui Resorts... 58
        Maui Weddings.. 62
        Surfing on Maui 63
        Snorkeling and Scuba on Maui 68
        Whale Watching on Maui 72
        Maui Historic Places 75
    By Region... 80
        Central Maui 80
            Wailuku.. 80
            Iao Valley State Park, Maui 82
        East Maui 83
            Hana, Maui.. 83
            Pools of Oheo, Maui 84
        South Maui 85

- Makena Beach State Park (Big Beach) 86
- Molokini 87
- Wailea 87
- Kihei 89
- Upcountry Maui 91
  - Paia, Maui 91
  - Haleakala National Park Maui 92
  - Kula 95
  - Makawao, Maui 97
- West Maui 98
  - Honolua Bay Maui 99
  - Lahaina, Maui 100
  - Kapalua Maui 102
  - Kaanapali Beach 103

Food & Drink *104*
Life & Language *113*
Restaurants *116*
Nightlife *118*
- The Entertainment Scene 124

Shopping *128*
Environment *134*
Planning a Trip *154*
- Entry Requirements & Customs 159
- Getting Around 165
- Fast Facts 168
- When to Go 170
- The Island in Brief 173
- Calendar of Events 186
- Tips on Accommodations 198
- Getting There 203
- Escorted & Package Tours 207
- Getting Married 212
- Sustainable Travel & Ecotourism 215
- Money 224
- Money 225
- Health & Safety 226
- Tips for Families 235
- Tips for Gay and Lesbian Travelers 236
- Tips for Senior Travelers 236
- Tips for Travelers with Disabilities 237

Walking Tours *238*

Driving Tours	252
The Road to Hana	255
Important Information	270
The Best Luxury Hotels	270
The Best Mid-Range Hotels	273
Best Dining Bets	275
The Best Shopping	281
The Best Adventures	284
The Best Resorts & Spas	286
vvvvvvv	288
The Best of Underwater Maui	288
The Best Beaches	290
The Best Golf Courses	293
The Best Inns and Bed & Breakfasts	295

Touristic Introduction

For many, Maui inhabits the sweet spot. It's a tangle of lovely contradictions, with a Gucci heel on one foot and a puka-shell anklet on the other. Culturally, it's a mix of farmers, paniolo (Hawaiian cowboys), aspiring chefs, artists, New Age healers, and big wave riders. The landscape runs the gamut from sun-kissed golden beaches and fragrant rainforests to the frigid, wind-swept summit of Haleakala. Sure, more traffic lights sprout up around the island every year and spurts of development have turned cherished landmarks into mere memories. But even as Maui transforms, its allure remains.

The Island in Brief
This medium-sized island lies in the center of the Hawaiian archipelago.

Central Maui
Maui, the Valley Isle, is so named for the large isthmus between the island's two towering volcanoes: Haleakala and the West Maui

Mountains. The flat landscape in between, Central Maui, is the heart of the island's business community and local government.

Kahului--Most Maui visitors fly over waving sugarcane fields to land at Kahului Airport, just yards away from rolling surf. Sadly, your first sight out of the airport will likely be a Costco—hardly an icon of Hawaiiana but always bustling with islanders and visitors alike. Beyond that, Kahului is a grid of shops and no-nonsense neighborhoods that you'll pass through en route to your destination.

Wailuku--Nestled up against the West Maui Mountains, Wailuku is a time capsule of faded wooden storefronts, old churches, and plantation homes. While most people zip through on their way to see the natural beauty of Iao Valley, this quaint little town is worth a brief visit, if only to see a real place where real people actually appear to be working at something other than a suntan. This is the county seat, so you'll see folks in suits (or at least aloha shirts and long pants) on important missions in the tropical heat. The town has some great budget restaurants, interesting bungalow architecture, a wonderful historic B&B, and the intriguing Bailey House Museum.

West Maui
Jagged peaks, velvety green valleys, a wilderness full of native species: The majestic West Maui Mountains are the epitome of earthly

paradise. The beaches below are crowded with condos and resorts, but still achingly beautiful. This stretch of coastline along Maui's "forehead," from Kapalua to the historic port of Lahaina, is the island's busiest resort area (with South Maui close behind). Expect slow-moving traffic on the two main thoroughfares: Honoapiilani Highway and Front Street.

Vacationers on this coast can choose from several beachside neighborhoods, each with its own identity and microclimate. The West Side tends to be hot, humid, and sunny year-round. As you travel north, the weather grows cooler and mistier. Starting at the southern end of West Maui and moving northward, the coastal communities look like this:

Lahaina--In days past, Lahaina was the seat of Hawaiian royalty. Legend has it that a powerful moʻo (lizard goddess) dwelt in a moat surrounding a palace here. Later, this hot and sunny seaport was where raucous whalers swaggered ashore in search of women and grog. Modern Lahaina is a tame version of its former self. Today Front Street teems with restaurants, T-shirt shops, and galleries. Action revolves around the town's giant, century-old banyan tree and busy recreational harbor. Parts of Lahaina are downright tacky, but you can still find plenty of authentic history here. It's also a great place to stay;

accommodations include a few old hotels (such as the 1901 Pioneer Inn on the harbor), quaint bed-and-breakfasts, and a handful of oceanfront condos.

Kaanapali--Farther north along the West Maui coast is Hawaii's first master-planned destination resort. Along nearly 3 miles of sun-kissed golden beach, pricey midrise hotels are linked by a landscaped parkway and a beachfront walking path. Golf greens wrap around the slope between beachfront and hillside properties.Convenience is a factor here: Whalers Village shopping mall and numerous restaurants are easy to reach on foot or by resort shuttle. Shuttles serves the small West Maui airport just to the north and also go to Lahainaah, for shopping, dining, entertainment, and boat tours. Kaanapali is popular with groups and families—and especially teenagers, who like all the action.

Honokowai, Kahana--In the building binge of the 1970s, condominiums sprouted along this gorgeous coastline like mushrooms after a rain. Today, these older oceanside units offer excellent bargains for astute travelers. The great location—along sandy beaches, within minutes of both the Kapalua and Kaanapali resort areas, and close enough to the goings-on in Lahaina town—makes this area a haven for the budget-minded.

In Honokowai and Mahinahina, you'll find mostly older, cheaper units. There's not much shopping here (mostly convenience stores), but you'll have easy access to the shops and restaurants of Kaanapali. Kahana is a little more upscale than Honokowai and Mahinahina, and most of its condos are big high-rise types, newer than those immediately to the south.

Napili--A quiet, tucked-away gem, with temperatures at least 5 degrees cooler than in Lahaina, this tiny neighborhood feels like a world unto itself. Wrapped around deliciously calm Napili Bay, Napili offers convenient activity desks and decent eateries and is close to the gourmet restaurants of Kapalua. Lodging is generally more expensive here—although I've found a few hidden jewels at affordable prices.

Kapalua--Beyond the activity of Kaanapali and Kahana, the road starts to climb and the vista opens up to include unfettered views of Molokai across the channel. A country lane lined with Cook pines brings you to Kapalua. It's the exclusive domain of the luxurious Ritz-Carlton resort and expensive condos and villas, set above two sandy beaches. Just north are two jeweled bays: marine-life preserves and world-class surf spot in winter. Although rain is frequent here, it doesn't dampen the enjoyment of this wilder stretch of coast.

Anyone is welcome to visit Kapalua, guest of the resort or not. The Ritz-Carlton provides free public parking and beach access. The resort has swank restaurants, spas, golf courses, and hiking trails—all open to the general public.

South Maui
The hot, sunny South Maui coastline is popular with families and sun worshippers. Rain rarely falls here, and temperatures hover around 85[dg]F (29[dg]C) year-round. Cows once grazed and cacti grew wild on this former scrubland from Maalaea to Makena, now home to four distinct areas—Maalaea, Kihei, Wailea, and Makena. Maalaea is off on its own, at the mouth of an active small boat harbor, Kihei is the working-class, feeder community for well-heeled Wailea, and Makena is a luxurious wilderness at the road's end.

Maalaea--If West Maui is the island's head, Maalaea is just under the chin. This windy, oceanfront village centers on a small-boat harbor (with a general store and a handful of restaurants) and the Maui Ocean Center, an aquarium/ocean complex. Visitors should be aware that tradewinds are near constant here, so a stroll on the beach often comes with a free sandblasting.

Kihei--Kihei is less a proper town than a nearly continuous series of condos and mini-malls lining South Kihei Road. This is Maui's best vacation bargain. Budget travelers swarm like sun-seeking geckos over the eight sandy beaches along this scalloped, 7-mile stretch of coast. Kihei is neither charming nor quaint; what it lacks in aesthetics, though, it more than makes up for in sunshine, affordability, and convenience. If you want the beach in the morning, shopping in the afternoon, and Hawaii Regional Cuisine in the evening—all at bargain prices—head to Kihei.

Wailea--Just 4 decades ago, the road south of Kihei was a barely paved path through a tangle of kiawe trees. Now Wailea is a manicured oasis of multimillion-dollar resorts along 2 miles of palm-fringed gold coast. Wailea has warm, clear water full of tropical fish; year-round sunshine and clear blue skies; and hedonistic pleasure palaces on 1,500 acres of black-lava shore indented by five beautiful beaches, each one prettier than the next.

This is the playground of the stretch-limo set. The planned resort development has a shopping village, a plethora of award-winning restaurants, several prized golf courses, and a tennis complex. A growing number of large homes sprawl over the upper hillside, some offering excellent B&Bs at reasonable prices. The resorts along this fantasy coast are spectacular. Next door to the Four Seasons Resort Maui at Wailea, the most elegant, is the Grand Wailea, built by Tokyo developer Takeshi Sekiguchi, who dropped $500 million in 1991 to create the most opulent Hawaiian resort to date. Stop in and take a look—sculptures by Botero and Leger populate its open-air art gallery and gardens. Stones imported from Mount Fuji line the Japanese garden fronting the resort's Amasia restaurant.

Makena--Suddenly, the road enters raw wilderness. After Wailea's overdone density, the thorny landscape is a welcome relief. Although beautiful, this is an end-of-the-road kind of place: It's a long drive from Makena to anywhere on Maui. If you're looking for an activity-filled vacation, stay elsewhere, or you'll spend most of your vacation in the car. But if you want a quiet, relaxing respite, where the biggest trip of the day is from your bed to the beach, Makena is the place.

Puu Olai stands like Maui's Diamond Head near the southern tip of the island. The red cinder cone shelters tropical fish and Makena State Beach Park, a vast stretch of golden sand spanked by feisty swells. Beyond Makena, you'll discover Haleakala's most recent lava flow; the bay named for French explorer La Pérouse; and a sunbaked lava-rock trail known as the King's Highway, which threads around Maui's southernmost shore through the ruins of bygone fishing villages.

Upcountry Maui

After a few days at the beach, you'll probably notice the 10,023-foot mountain towering over Maui. The leeward slopes of Haleakala (House of the Sun) are home to cowboys, farmers, and other rural folks who wave as you drive by. They're all up here enjoying the crisp air, emerald pastures, eucalyptus, and flower farms of this tropical Olympus. The neighborhoods here are called "upcountry" because they're halfway up the mountain. You can see a thousand tropical sunsets reflected in the windows of houses old and new, strung along a road that runs like a loose hound from Makawao to Kula, leading up to the summit and Haleakala National Park. If you head south on Kula Highway, beyond the tiny outpost of Keokea, the road turns feral, undulating out towards Tedeschi Winery, where grapes, cattle, and elk flourish on Ulupalakua Ranch. A stay upcountry is usually affordable and a nice contrast to the sizzling beaches and busy resorts below.

Makawao--This small, two-street town has plenty of charm. It wasn't long ago that Hawaiian paniolo (cowboys) tied up their horses to the hitching posts outside the storefronts here; working ranchers still stroll through to pick up coffee and packages from the post office. The eclectic shops, galleries, and restaurants have a little something for everyone—from blocked Stetsons to wind chimes. Nearby, the Hui No'eau Visual Arts Center, Hawaii's premier arts collective, is definitely worth a detour. Makawao's only accommodations are reasonably priced bed-and-breakfasts, perfect for those who love great views and don't mind slightly chilly nights.

Kula--A feeling of pastoral remoteness prevails in this upcountry community of old flower farms, humble cottages, and new suburban ranch houses with million-dollar views that take in the ocean, the isthmus, the West Maui Mountains, and, at night, the lights that run along the gold coast like a string of pearls from Maalaea to Puu Olai. Everything flourishes at a cool 3,000 feet (bring a jacket), just below the cloud line, along a winding road on the way up to Haleakala National Park. Everyone here grows something—Maui onions, lavender, orchids, and proteas—and B&Bs cater to guests seeking cool tropical nights, panoramic views, and a rural upland escape. Here you'll find the true peace and quiet that only rural farming country can offer—yet you're still just 30 to 40 minutes away from the beach and an hour's drive from Lahaina.

On the Road to Hana--On Maui's north shore, Paia was once a busy sugar plantation town, with a railroad, two movie theaters, and a double-decker mercantile. As the sugar industry began to wane, the tuned-in, dropped-out hippies of the 1970s moved in, followed shortly by a cosmopolitan collection of windsurfers. When the international wave riders discovered Hookipa Beach Park just outside of town, their minds were blown; it's one of the best places on the planet to catch air. Today, high-tech windsurf shops, trendy restaurants, bikini boutiques, and modern art galleries inhabit Paia's rainbow-colored vintage buildings. The Dalai Lama himself blessed the beautiful Tibetan stupa in the center of town. Mama's Fish House is located east of Paia, in the tiny community of Kuau.

Ten minutes farther east is Haiku. Once a pineapple plantation village, complete with two canneries (both now shopping complexes), Haiku offers vacation rentals and B&Bs in a pastoral setting. It's the perfect base for those who want to get off the beaten path and experience the quieter side of Maui.

Hana--Set between an emerald rainforest and the blue Pacific is a Hawaiian village blissfully lacking in golf courses, shopping malls, and fast-food joints. Hana is more of a sensory overload than a destination; here you'll discover the simple joys of rain-misted flowers, the sweet taste of backyard bananas and papayas, and the easy calm and unabashed aloha spirit of old Hawaii. What saved "Heavenly" Hana from the inevitable march of progress? The 52-mile Hana Highway, which winds around 600 curves and crosses more than 50 one-lane bridges on its way from Kahului. You can go to Hana for the day—it's 3 hours (and a half-century) from Kihei and Lahaina—but 3 days are better

History

Paddling outrigger canoes, the first ancestors of today's Hawaiians followed the stars and birds across the sea to Hawaii, which they called "the land of raging fire." Those first settlers were part of the great Polynesian migration that settled the vast triangle of islands stretching between New Zealand, Easter Island, and Hawaii. No one is sure exactly when they came to Hawaii from Tahiti and the Marquesas Islands, some 2,500 miles to the south, but a bone fishhook found at the southernmost tip of the Big Island has been carbon-dated to A.D. 700. Chants claim that the Mookini Heiau, also on the Big Island, was built in A.D. 480. Some recent archaeological digs at Maluuluolele Park in Lahaina even predate that.

All we have today are some archaeological finds, some scientific data, and ancient chants to tell the story of Hawaii's past. The chants, especially the *Kumulipo,* which is the chant of creation and the litany of genealogy of the *alii* (high-ranking chiefs) who ruled the islands, talk about comings and goings between Hawaii and the islands of the south, presumed to be Tahiti. In fact, the channel between Maui, Kahoolawe, and Lanai is called *Kealaikahiki,* or "the pathway to Tahiti."

Around 1300, the transoceanic voyages stopped for some reason, and Hawaii began to develop its own culture in earnest. The settlers built temples, fish ponds, and aqueducts to irrigate taro plantations. Sailors became farmers and fishermen. Each island was a separate kingdom. The *alii* created a caste system and established taboos. Violators were strangled. High priests asked the gods Lono and Ku for divine guidance. Ritual human sacrifices were common.

Maui's history, like that of the rest of Hawaii, is one of wars and conquests, with one king taking over another king's land. The rugged terrain of Maui and the water separating Maui, Molokai, Lanai, and Kahoolawe made for natural boundaries of kingdoms. In the early years, there were three kingdoms on Maui: Hana, Waikulu, and Lahaina. The chants are not just strict listings of family histories. Some describe how a ruler's pride and arrogance can destroy a community. For example, according to the chants, Hana's King Hua killed a priest in the 12th century, and as a result the gods sent a severe drought to Hana as a punishment.

Three centuries later, another ruler came out of Hana who would change the course of Maui's history: Piilani, the first ruler to unite all of Maui. His rule was a time not only of peace but also of community construction projects. Piilani built fish ponds and irrigation fields and began creating a paved road some 4 to 6 feet wide around the entire island. Piilani's sons and grandson continued these projects and completed the *Alalou,*the royal road that circled the united island. They also completed Hawaii's largest *heiau*(temple) to the god of war, Piilanihale, which still stands today.

Maui was a part of a pivotal change in Hawaii's history: After conquering Maui in 1795, Kamehameha united all of the islands into one kingdom. It started in 1759, when yet another battle over land was going on. This time Kalaniopuu, a chief from the Big Island, had captured Hana from the powerful Maui chief Kahikili. Kahikili was busy overtaking Molokai when the Big Island chief stole Hana from him. The Molokai chief escaped and fled with his wife to Hana, where the Big Island chief welcomed him. A few years later, the Molokai chief and his wife had a baby girl in Hana, named Kaahumanu, who later married Kamehameha.

The "Fatal Catastrophe" No ancient Hawaiian ever imagined a *haole* (a white person; literally, one with "no breath") would ever appear on one of these "floating islands." But then one day in 1778, just such a person sailed into Waimea Bay on Kauai, where he was welcomed as the god Lono.

The man was 50-year-old Capt. James Cook, already famous in Britain for "discovering" much of the South Pacific. Now on his third great voyage of exploration, Cook had set sail from Tahiti northward across uncharted waters to find the mythical Northwest Passage that was said to link the Pacific and Atlantic oceans. On his way, Cook stumbled upon the Hawaiian Islands quite by chance. He named them the Sandwich Islands, for the Earl of Sandwich, first lord of the admiralty, who had bankrolled the expedition.

Overnight, Stone Age Hawaii entered the age of iron. Nails were traded for fresh water, pigs, and the affections of Hawaiian women. The sailors brought syphilis, measles, and other diseases to which the Hawaiians had no natural immunity, thereby unwittingly wreaking havoc on the native population.

After his unsuccessful attempt to find the Northwest Passage, Cook returned to Kealakekua Bay on the Big Island, where a fight broke out over an alleged theft, and the great navigator was killed by a blow to the head. After this "fatal catastrophe," the British survivors sailed home. But Hawaii was now on the sea charts, and traders on the fur route between Canada and China anchored in Hawaii to get fresh water. More trade and more disastrous liaisons ensued.

Two more sea captains left indelible marks on the islands. The first was American John Kendrick, who in 1791 filled his ship with sandalwood and sailed to China. By 1825, Hawaii's sandalwood forests were gone, enabling invasive plants to take charge. The second captain was Englishman George Vancouver, who in 1793 left cows and sheep, which spread out to the high-tide lines. King Kamehameha I sent for cowboys from Mexico and Spain to round up the wild livestock, thus beginning the islands' *paniolo*(cowboy) tradition.

The tightly woven Hawaiian society began to unravel after the death in 1819 of King Kamehameha I, who had used guns seized from a British ship to unite the islands under his rule. One of his successors, Queen Kaahumanu, abolished old taboos, such as that of women eating with men, and opened the door for religion of another form when she converted to Christianity.

Staying To Do Well In 1819, the first whaling ship dropped anchor in Lahaina. Sailors on the *Bellina* were looking for fresh water and supplies, but they found beautiful women, mind-numbing grog, and a tropical paradise. A few years later, in 1823, the whalers met rivals for this hedonistic playground: the missionaries. The God-fearing missionaries arrived from New England bent on converting the pagans. They chose Lahaina because it was the capital of Hawaii.

Intent on instilling their brand of rock-ribbed Christianity in the islands, the missionaries clothed the natives, banned them from dancing the hula, and nearly dismantled their ancient culture. They tried to keep the whalers and sailors out of the bawdy houses, where a flood of whiskey quenched fleet-size thirsts and where the virtue of native women was never safe.

The missionaries taught reading and writing, created the 12-letter Hawaiian alphabet, started a printing press in Lahaina, and began writing the islands' history, which until then had existed only as an oral account in memorized chants. They also started the first school in Lahaina, which still exists today: the Lahainaluna High School.

Children of the missionaries became the islands' business leaders and politicians. They married Hawaiians and stayed on in the islands, causing one wag to remark that the missionaries "came to do good and stayed to do well."

In Lahaina's heyday, some 500 whaling ships a year dropped anchor in the Lahaina Roadstead. In 1845, King Kamehameha III moved the capital of Hawaii from Lahaina to Honolulu, where more commerce could be accommodated in the natural harbor there. Some whaling ships started skipping Lahaina for the larger port of Honolulu. Fifteen years later, the depletion of whales and the emergence of petroleum as a more suitable oil signaled the beginning of the end of the whaling industry.

King Sugar Emerges When the capital of Hawaii moved to Honolulu, Maui might have taken a back seat in Hawaii's history had it not been for the beginning of a new industry: sugar. In 1849, George Wilfong, a cantankerous sea captain, built a mill in Hana and planted some 60 acres of sugar cane, creating Hawaii's first sugar plantation. At that time, the gold rush was on in California, and sugar prices were wildly inflated. Wilfong's harsh personality and the demands he placed on plantation workers did not sit well with the Hawaiians. In 1852, he imported Chinese immigrants to work in his fields. By the end of the 1850s, the gold rush had begun to diminish, and the inflated sugar prices dropped. When Wilfong's mill burned down, he finally called it quits.

Sugar production continued in Hana, however. In 1864, two Danish brothers, August and Oscar Unna, started the Hana Plantation. Four years later they imported Japanese immigrants to work the fields.

Some 40 miles away, in Haiku, two sons of missionaries, Samuel Alexander and Henry Baldwin, planted 12 acres of this new crop. The next year, Alexander and Baldwin added some 5,000 acres in Maui's central plains and started Hawaii's largest sugar company. They quickly discovered that without the copious amounts of rainfall found in Hana, they would need to get water to their crop, or it would fail. In 1876, they constructed an elaborate ditch system that brought water from rainy Haiku some 17 miles away to the dry plains of Wailuku, a move that cemented the future of sugar in Hawaii.

Around the same time, another sugar pioneer, Claus Spreckels, bought up property in the arid desert of Puunene from Hawaiians who sold him the "cursed" lands at a very cheap price. The Hawaiians were sure they had gotten the better part of the deal because they believed that the lands were haunted.

Spreckels was betting that these "cursed" lands could be very productive if he could get water rights up in the rainy hills and bring that water to Puunene, just as Alexander and Baldwin had done. But first he needed that water. Thus began a series of late-night poker games with the then-king Kalakaua. Spreckels's gamble paid off: Not only did he beat the king at poker (some say he cheated), but he also built the elaborate 30-mile Haiku Ditch system, which transported 50 million gallons of water a day from rainy Haiku to dry Puunene.

The big boost to sugar, not only on Maui but also across the entire state, came in 1876, when King Kalakaua negotiated the Sugar Reciprocity Treaty with the United States, giving the Hawaiian sugar industry a "sweet" deal on prices and tariffs.

In 1891, King Kalakaua visited chilly San Francisco, caught a cold, and died in the royal suite of the Sheraton Palace. His sister, Queen Liliuokalani, assumed the throne.

A Sad Farewell On January 17, 1893, a group of American sugar planters and missionary descendants, with the support of U.S. Marines, imprisoned Queen Liliuokalani in her own palace, where she later penned the sorrowful lyric "Aloha Oe," Hawaii's song of farewell. The monarchy was dead.

A new republic was established, controlled by Sanford Dole, a powerful sugar-cane planter. In 1898, through annexation, Hawaii became an American territory ruled by Dole. His fellow sugar-cane planters, known as the Big Five, controlled banking, shipping, hardware, and every other facet of economic life on the islands.

Planters imported more contract laborers from Puerto Rico (in 1900), Korea (in 1903), and the Philippines (1907-31). Most of the new immigrants stayed on to establish families and become a part of the islands. Meanwhile, the native Hawaiians became a landless minority in their homeland.

For nearly a century on Hawaii, sugar was king, generously subsidized by the U.S. federal government. The sugar planters dominated the territory's economy, shaped its social fabric, and kept the islands in a colonial plantation era with bosses and field hands.

World War II & Its Aftermath On December 7, 1941, Japanese Zeros came out of the rising sun to bomb American warships based at Pearl Harbor, on the island of Oahu. This was the "day of infamy" that plunged the United States into World War II.

The attack brought immediate changes to the islands. Martial law was declared, stripping the Big Five cartel of its absolute power in a single day. Japanese Americans and German Americans were interned. Hawaii was "blacked out" at night, Waikiki Beach was strung with barbed wire, and Aloha Tower was painted in camouflage.

During the postwar years, the men of Hawaii returned after seeing another, bigger world outside of plantation life and rebelled. Throwing off the mantle of plantation life, the workers struck for higher wages and improved working conditions. Within a few short years after the war, the white, Republican leaders who had ruled since the overthrow of the monarchy were voted out of office, and labor leaders in the Democratic Party were suddenly in power.

Tourism & Statehood In 1959, Hawaii became the 50th state of the union. But that year also saw the arrival of the first jet airliners, which brought 250,000 tourists to the fledgling state.

Tourism had already started on Maui shortly after World War II, when Paul I. Fagan, an entrepreneur from San Francisco who had bought the Hana Sugar Co., became the town's angel.

Fagan wanted to retire to Hana, so he focused his business acumen on this tiny town with big problems. Years ahead of his time, he thought tourism might have a future in Hana, so he built a small six-room inn, called Kauiki Inn, which later became the Hotel Hana-Maui. When he opened it in 1946, he said it was for first-class, wealthy travelers (just like his friends). Not only did his friends come, but he also pulled off a public-relations coup that is still talked about today. Fagan owned a baseball team, the San Francisco Seals. He figured they needed a spring-training area, so why not use Hana? He brought out the entire team to train in Hana, and, more important, he brought out the sportswriters. The sportswriters penned glowing reports about the town, and one writer gave the town a name that stuck: "Heavenly Hana."

However, it would be another 3 decades before Maui became a popular visitor destination in Hawaii. Waikiki was king in the tourism industry, seeing some 16,000 visitors a year by the end of the 1960s, and some 4 million a year by the end of the 1970s. In 1960, Amfac, owner of Pioneer Sugar Co., looked at the area outside of Lahaina that was being used to dump sugar-cane refuse and saw another use for the beachfront land. The company decided to build a manicured, planned luxury resort in the Kaanapali area. They built it, and people came.

A decade later, Alexander & Baldwin, now the state's largest sugar company, looked at the arid land they owned south of Kihei and also saw possibilities: The resort destination of Wailea was born.

By the mid-1970s, some one million visitors a year were coming to Maui. Ten years later, the number was up to two million.

At the beginning of the 21st century, the visitor industry replaced agriculture as Maui's number-one industry. Maui is the second-largest visitor destination in Hawaii. For 13 years in a row, the readers of *Condé Nast Traveler* and *Travel + Leisure* magazines have voted Maui the "Best Island in the World."

Hawaii was at record-breaking visitor counts (6.9 million) in 2000. Then on September 11, 2001, terrorists attacked the mainland and tourism dropped abruptly in Hawaii, sending the state's economy into a tailspin. But people eventually started traveling again, and in 2003, visitor arrivals were up to 6.3 million. By 2005, Hawaii's economy was recovering, the number of visitors to the state shot up to 6.75 million, business was booming in construction, and real-estate sales were higher than ever.

Just 3 years later, the economic pendulum swung the opposite way. Real estate in Hawaii, as on the mainland, dropped in value and sales plummeted. A record number of visitors, some nine million, had come to Hawaii in 2007, but the economic downturn in 2008 caused the closure of Aloha Airlines (which had served Hawaii for 61 years) and ATA Airlines, as well as Molokai Ranch, that island's largest employer and landowner.

After more than a decade in the new century, Maui is still climbing out of the recession and the tourism industry has not yet recovered to its former healthy state.

Maui Arts & Culture

From the forces of King Kamehameha defeating King Kahekili in Iao Valley to the rowdy whalers of 19th century Lahaina, this island's intangible mystique has been drawing visitors throughout history.

To step back in Maui's past, visit the Whalers Village Museum for an historic account of the whaling industry, discover Maui's agricultural past at the Alexander & Baldwin Sugar Museum or follow the Lahaina Historic Trail to explore this thriving seaport's heritage.

Today, Maui reveals its cultural past through a thriving arts scene infused with the life-embracing spirit of aloha. From the events and exhibitions at the Maui Arts and Cultural Center and the Hui Noeau Visual Arts Center to Art Night every Friday in Lahaina, Maui continues to pay homage to its rich history. Local artists and artisans are also expanding their influence by creating a wide range of products, from hip fashion to traditional and contemporary crafts.

Atmosphere

Since the Polynesians ventured across the Pacific to the Hawaiian Islands more than 1,000 years ago, these floating jewels have continued to call visitors from around the globe.

Located in one of the most remote and isolated places on the planet, Maui, as part of the Hawaiian Islands chain, floats in the warm waters of the Pacific, blessed by a tropical sun and cooled by gentle year-round trade winds creating what might be the most ideal climate imaginable. Centuries of the indigenous Hawaiian culture have given the people of the islands the "spirit of aloha," a warm, welcoming attitude that invites visitors to come and share this exotic paradise. Mother Nature has carved out verdant valleys, hung brilliant rainbows in the sky, and trimmed the islands with sandy beaches in a spectrum of colors, from white to black to even green and red.

Visitors are drawn to Maui not only for its incredible beauty, but also for its opportunities for adventure: bicycling down a 10,000-foot dormant volcano, swimming in a sea of rainbow-colored fish, hiking into a rainforest, or watching whales leap out of the ocean as you tee off on one of the country's top golf courses. Others come to rest and relax in a land where the pace of life moves at a slower rate and the sun's rays soothe and allow both body and mind to regenerate and recharge.

Venturing to Maui is not your run-of-the-mill vacation, but rather an experience in the senses that will remain with you, locked into your memory, way, way, way after your tan fades. Years later, a sweet smell, the warmth of the sun on your body, or the sound of the wind through the trees will take you back to the time you spent in the islands.

Incidentally, Maui is the only island in the Hawaiian chain named after a god well, actually a demigod (half man, half god). Hawaiian legends are filled with the escapades of Maui, who had a reputation as a trickster. In one story, Maui is credited with causing the birth of the Hawaiian Islands when he threw his "magic" fishhook down to the ocean floor and pulled the islands up from the bottom of the sea. Another legend tells how Maui lassoed the sun to make it travel more slowly across the sky so that his mother could more easily dry her clothes. Maui's status as the only island to carry the name of a deity seems fitting, considering its reputation as the perfect tropical paradise, or as Hawaiians say, *Maui no ka oi.* (Maui is the best.)

A Cultural Renaissance A conch shell sounds, a young man in a bright feather cape chants, torchlight flickers at sunset on the beach, and hula dancers begin telling their graceful centuries-old stories. It's a cultural scene out of the past come to life once again for Hawaii is enjoying a renaissance of hula, chant, and other aspects of its ancient culture.

The biggest, longest, and most elaborate celebrations of Hawaiian culture are the Aloha Festivals, which encompass more than 500 cultural events from August to October. "Our goal is to teach and share our culture," says Gloriann Akau, a former manager of the Aloha Festivals. "In 1946, after the war, Hawaiians needed an identity. We were lost and needed to regroup. When we started to celebrate our culture, we began to feel proud. We have a wonderful culture that had been buried for a number of years. This brought it out again. Self-esteem is more important than making a lot of money."

In 1985, native Hawaiian educator, author, and *kupuna* (respected elder) George Kanahele started integrating Hawaiian values into hotels like Maui's Kaanapali Beach Hotel. "You have the responsibility to preserve and enhance the Hawaiian culture, not because it's going to make money for you, but because it's the right thing to do," Kanahele told the Hawaii Hotel Association. "Ultimately, the only thing unique about Hawaii is its Hawaiianess. Hawaiianess is our competitive edge."

From general managers to maids, resort employees went through hours of Hawaiian cultural training. They held focus groups to discuss the meaning of aloha the Hawaiian concept of unconditional love and applied it to their work and their lives. Now many hotels have joined the movement and instituted Hawaiian programs. No longer content with teaching hula as a joke, resorts now employ a real *kumu hula* (hula teacher) to instruct visitors and have a *kupuna* (elder) take guests on treks to visit *heiau*(temples) and ancient petroglyph sites.

The Question of Sovereignty The Hawaiian cultural renaissance has also made its way into politics. Many *kanaka maoli* (native people) are demanding restoration of rights taken away more than a century ago when the U.S. overthrew the Hawaiian monarchy. Their demands were not lost on President Bill Clinton, who was picketed at a Democratic political fundraiser at Waikiki Beach in July 1993. Four months later, Clinton signed a document stating that the U.S. Congress "apologizes to Native Hawaiians on behalf of the people of the United States for the overthrow of the Kingdom of Hawaii on January 17, 1893, with the participation of agents and citizens of the United States, and deprivation of the rights of Native Hawaiians to self-determination."

But even neonationalists aren't convinced that complete self-determination is possible. Each of the 30 identifiable sovereignty organizations (and more than 100 splinter groups) has a different stated goal, ranging from total independence to nation-within-a-nation status, similar to that of Native Americans. In 1993, the state legislature created a Hawaiian Sovereignty Advisory Commission to "determine the will of the native Hawaiian people." The commission plans to pose the sovereignty question in a referendum open to all persons over age 18 with Hawaiian blood, no matter where they live. The question still remains unanswered.

Symbol of a Culture: The Outrigger Canoe

Hawaiians have been masters of the outrigger canoe since the first Polynesians landed on the islands' shores about 1,500 years ago. Today, outrigger canoeing is the official state sport, and dozens of canoeing clubs throughout the islands cater to a growing interest and pride in this oldest of Hawaiian traditions.

Far more than a simple mode of transportation, the canoe in ancient Hawaii was inextricably woven into the culture: as an expression of royal power, the basis of its early naval fleet, a favorite sport, an essential tool for fishing and survival, and an art form. Outrigger canoes have one or more lateral support floats (outriggers), or can be double-hulled, like today's catamarans. Historically, the one-piece hulls were carved from the hardwood koa tree; the floats and other parts were lashed together with coconut-fiber cord. Sails were mats woven from pandanus leaves. Because the canoe's performance in Hawaii's rough ocean waters could determine life or death, a priest often oversaw the building of the vessel, and offerings of fish, pigs, and flowers were made upon completion of a canoe. Canoe racing was a physically rigorous sport, and races were held primarily for serious gambling purposes. It's estimated that when the Europeans arrived in the eighteenth century there were as many as 12,000 canoes in Hawaii, though canoe racing, like surfing, was banned once missionaries arrived, around 1820.

Centuries before European explorers were plying the world's oceans, the Hawaiians' ancestors, the Polynesians, were using sophisticated long-distance navigation techniques and large, double-hulled outrigger canoes to travel thousands of miles in the vast Pacific. From their earliest origins in Southeast Asia, these early navigators traveled to the western edge of Polynesia (Micronesia) between 3,000 and 1,500 B.C. From there, they steadily moved west and north to colonize eastern Polynesian islands like Samoa and Tonga. Sometime between 300 and 700 A.D., the Polynesians arrived in New Zealand, the Easter Islands (Rapa Nui), and Hawaii. The Polynesians and Hawaiians practiced star map navigation, which uses the rising points of the stars, and observation of the sun, moon, ocean swells, and flight patterns of birds, as a natural compass to steer the course.

The Lei of the Land

There's nothing like a lei: the stunning tropical beauty of the delicate garland, the deliciously sweet fragrance of the blossoms, the sensual way the flowers curl softly around your neck. There's no doubt about it: Getting lei'd in Hawaii is a sensuous experience. Leis are one of the nicest ways to say hello, good-bye, congratulations, I salute you, my sympathies are with you, or I love you. The custom of giving leis can be traced back to Hawaii's very roots; according to chants, the first lei was given by Hiiaka, the sister of the volcano goddess Pele, who presented Pele with a lei of lehua blossoms on a beach in Puna.

The presentation of a kiss with a lei didn't come about until World War II; it's generally attributed to an entertainer who kissed an officer on a dare and then quickly presented him with her lei, saying it was an old Hawaiian custom. Leis are the perfect symbol for the islands: They're given in the moment and their fragrance and beauty are enjoyed in the moment, but even after they fade, their spirit of aloha lives on. Lei making is a tropical art form. All leis are fashioned by hand in a variety of traditional patterns; some are sewn with hundreds of tiny blooms or shells, or bits of ferns and leaves. Some are twisted, some braided, some strung; all are presented with love. The lei of choice on Maui is the lokelani, a small rose. Molokai's specialty lei is the kukui, the white blossom of a candlenut tree. On Lanai, it's the kaunaoa, a bright yellow moss.

Festivals of Maui

Festivals and Annual Events on Maui
There's always something happening on Maui. Attending one of the Magic Isle's lively festivals is a great way to experience its diverse cultural heritage, sample its local cuisine and take in some rousing musical performances.

Cultural Festivals

Maui's cultural past, present and future are celebrated through a wide variety of events, like Olukai Hoolaulea (May)—a tribute to the ocean and the cultures that surround it—and the East Maui Taro Festival (April) in Hana, which honors Hawaii's "staff of life"; if you thought taro stopped at poi, wait til you try fluffy pancakes and more goodies made with Hawaii's most traditional food staple.

Food Festivals

Foodies will also love the Maui Onion Festival (May) and the long-running Kapalua Wine & Food Festival (June), a prestigious culinary event replete with internationally renowned winemakers, legendary sommeliers and top chefs. The Hawaii Food & Wine Festival (October) takes place on three islands including Maui, and features wine tastings, cooking demos and more.

Music and Film Festivals

The Hawaiian Slack Key Guitar Festival (June) in Central Maui honors an art form that originated in Hawaii nearly two centuries ago. Watch performances by more than a dozen masters of this musical style that has given Hawaiian culture a distinctive voice. Likewise, the Hawaiian Steel Guitar Festival (April) showcases its own "living treasures of Hawaiian music" in a series of free concerts, jam sessions and workshops. Film fans will enjoy the annual Maui Film Festival (June), which has drawn national acclaim for its premieres and screenings, many of which take place outdoors under a starry sky (talk about movie magic).

Travel and Tourism

About Maui

Stand above a sea of clouds high atop Haleakala. Watch a 45-foot whale breach off the coast of Lahaina. Lose count of the waterfalls along the road as you maneuver the hairpin turns of the Hana highway. One visit and it's easy to see why Maui is called "The Valley Isle."

The second largest Hawaiian island has a smaller population than you'd expect, making Maui popular with visitors who are looking for sophisticated diversions and amenities in the small towns and airy resorts spread throughout the island.

From the scenic slopes of fertile Upcountry Maui to beaches that have repeatedly been voted among the best in the world, a visit to the Valley Isle recharges the senses. But like every good magic trick, you'll have to see it for yourself to believe it.

Maui Travel Tips

Getting to Maui

Kahului Airport (OGG) is the Maui's main airport. There are two smaller commuter airports as well: Kapalua Airport (JHM) in West Maui and Hana Airport (HNM) in East Maui. Many airlines offer non-stop flights direct to Maui. You may also fly into Honolulu International Airport (HNL) on Oahu before heading to Maui on a short, 30-minute flight. There is also daily ferry service to and from the nearby islands of Lanai and Molokai.

Airport Travel Tips

- Check-in baggage is limited to 2 per person.

- Carry-on baggage is limited to one piece, along with one personal item such as notebook computer bags, purses, briefcases, cameras, etc.

- Be careful not to have overweight baggage; U.S. weight restrictions when flying domestically are 50 pounds, 70 pounds when flying internationally. The flight from the continental U.S. to Hawaii is a domestic flight.

- Hang identification tag on your baggage and affix an identifying label on your laptop.

- When departing from Hawaii, all baggage must first pass through Agriculture Quarantine before proceeding to the airline counter for check-in. It is best not to bring fruit or other plants, unless you show proof that you are allowed to export them. Without proof, fruits, vegetables and plants will not clear Customs and will be confiscated.

- Once you check-in for your flight, you must go through a security scan. You must have your boarding pass and identification or passport ready.

- Follow the recommended airport arrival and boarding time given by your airline or travel agency. It's always best to arrive at the airport early.

Staying on Maui

There are a wide range of accommodations on Maui, including high-end resorts, hotels, bed and breakfasts, and rentals. You'll find resorts and hotels in Kapalua, Kaanapali, Lahaina, Kihei, Makena and Wailea on Maui's sunny western coast as well as one resort in Hana in east Maui.

Anytime of year is a good time to visit Maui. The average temperature here is between 75-85 F. Summer, between April and November, is warmer and drier while winter, between December and March, is a bit cooler. Trade winds keep things comfortable year-round. It is generally drier on the western (leeward) side and wetter on the eastern (windward) side.

Traveling on Maui

You can get around Maui by shuttle, tour bus, taxi, or public transportation. But to really experience all that Maui offers you should consider reserving a rental car in advance from the Kahului or Kapalua Airport.

Currency ExchangeHawaii's currency is the U.S. dollar. You can exchange currency at Kahului Airport (OGG), at the other major neighbor island airports, and at resort destinations. Major credit cards are widely accepted and ATM machines are plentiful. Traveler's checks are accepted at many businesses.

What to Pack

It's warm in Hawaii, so pack your summer attire. You may want to bring a jacket or sweater for the evenings. Bring warmer clothes if you plan on visiting higher elevations like Haleakala National Park. Suits and ties are very rarely worn here. Bring some casual dress clothes or resort wear if you plan on experiencing Hawaii's nightlife. You can buy an aloha shirt and flip-flops (or slippers, as the locals call them) when you get here.

Tipping

U.S. standards on tipping apply:

- ➤ Restaurants: 15-20%. Check to see if "gratuity" is included for large parties

- ➤ Bar: $.50-$1 US per drink

- ➤ Housekeeping: $1 US per bed, per night

- ➤ Luggage porters: $1 US per bag

- ➤ Doorman: $1 US for calling a taxi

- ➤ Room Service: 10-15% of the total bill

- ➤ Taxi: 15% of fare

Language

The official languages of Hawaii are English and Hawaiian, although Hawaiian is not commonly spoken. Major resort areas often have customer service representatives who speak Japanese.

Internet and Electricity

Internet access is readily available in Hawaii. Electricity in the U.S. is 120 volts (120 v) at 60 cycles (60 Hz) per second. If your device does not accept this voltage, you may need to purchase a voltage converter.

Agricultural Inspection

The U.S. Department of Agriculture enforces strict rules regarding the exportation of uninspected plants and animals and requires a declaration form for each person arriving in Hawaii. When departing, your luggage must pass a pre-flight screening for uninspected fruits and plants. You are welcome to take inspected fresh flowers and fruits home. Items purchased at the airport or mailed home form local vendors are inspected for you.

Useful Phone Numbers and Links:

The area code for the state of Hawaii is (808)

Maui Visitors Bureau: (808) 525-MAUI (6284)

Kahului Airport Visitor Information: (808) 872-3893

Marriage License and Civil Unions: (808) 586-4545

Hospitals: Maui Memorial Medical Center: (808) 244-9056, Hana Community Health Center: (808) 248-8294

Maui Ecotourism

You don't need to be an environmentalist to appreciate the value of leaving a small footprint on the places you visit. In fact, you'd be in line with the Native Hawaiian concept of "malama aina" or caring for the land.

On Maui, respect for the land is an integral a part of our local lifestyle, whether it's dining on sustainable foods, preserving native plants and their many uses, or simply appreciating the gift that is our natural environment.

Take a drive to Upcountry Maui and you'll find yourself in Kula strolling among sweet fields of lavender and vibrant protea. Or walk back in time through gardens of indigenous plants at the Kula Botanical Garden. Continue to the 30,000-foot summit of Haleakala and you just might meet our state bird, the endangered nene (Hawaiian goose), or stumble across a Haleakala silversword, a rare and beautiful succulent that shimmers in the early light.

At the Iao Needle State Park in Central Maui, the mist descends upon the "needle" giving the historical site an almost mystical feeling, while the adjacent Nature Center offers an easy rainforest hike and a chance to learn about life in ancient Hawaii.

And at the heart, or should we stay the stomach, of Maui's sustainability efforts are the many island farms and ranches that produce the farm-to-table ingredients that grace our Hawaii Regional Cuisine. From chocolate to goat cheese to mountain-grown coffee, it's a gourmet's delight.

Where do you start? Maui offers many farm tours, as well as beaches, whale-watching and other activities. Or simply, take the road less traveled and see what you find.

Maui Adventures

On Maui, you'll have plenty of chances to try an array of outdoor adventures you've never experienced before. Snorkelers will be rewarded with unforgettable sights in Molokini's luminous waters. See your first humpback spout as you whale-watch from Kaanapali Beach. Or feel the rush of your first surf lesson off the shores of historic Lahaina.

On land, horseback ride atop Haleakala, Maui's highest peak. You can even take your first helicopter ride to see breathtaking views of Maui's pristine valleys and waterfalls.

Not enough time to do it all? You can always come back for more. For most visitors, their first adventures on this miraculous island are rarely their last.

Weather

Maui contains a number of microclimates. It is generally drier on Maui's leeward side where you'll find the spectacular beaches and resortsof Kapalua, Kaanapali, Lahaina, Kihei and Wailea along the western coast. On the wetter windward side you'll find lush Iao Valley and the scenic road to Hana. It's warmer along the coast than Upcountry Maui where temperatures are typically 8-10 degrees cooler. If you're driving up to the 9,740-foot Haleakala Visitor Center atop Haleakala National Park, expect temperatures in the 40s or lower, so bring warm clothes.

There are generally two seasons in Maui. Winter (November through April), when temperatures typically range in the low-70s to mid-80s, and summer when the high can run into the low-90s. The trade winds keep you comfortable year-round so any time of year is a good time to visit Maui.

Your First Trip to Maui

The thought of lying on sun soaked beaches regularly named "the best" by travel magazines is enough to make any of your friends jealous. But once you arrive on Maui, you'll see there's so much more for them to envy.

Most flights arrive at Maui's main airport, Kahului Airport (OGG). Many airlines fly direct to Maui while others include Maui as a stopover. You'll find resorts and hotels of every size and budget in Kapalua, Kaanapali, Lahaina, Kihei, Makena and Wailea on the sunny western coast as well as one resort in Hana in East Maui. It's about a 45-minute drive from Kahului Airport to Lahaina.

Once you've settled in you'll want to explore Maui's sweeping canvas of attractions. The western, or leeward side, is the drier side of the island and features Maui's world-famous beaches including the beautiful Kaanapali Beach, home to a nightly sunset cliff diving ceremony. West Maui is also home to historic Lahaina, where you can find great shopping, dining and entertainment.

The eastern, or windward side, of the island is the wetter side of the island, home to the lush Iao Valley and the scenic road to Hana. The cool, elevated slopes of Haleakala are where you can find the farms and gardens of Upcountry Maui and the soaring summit of Haleakala National Park. There is so much to see and do on Maui it's best to plan ahead. Just don't forget to send your friends a postcard.

Having Fun

Maui Romance

From watching an intimate sunrise, wrapped together in a blanket at the top of Haleakala Crater, to seeing the sunset as you cruise along the golden Kihei coastline, Maui is a place where romance isn't hard to find.

One of the top honeymoon destinations in the world, Maui's alluring beaches and immaculate resorts also provide an idyllic setting for weddings, receptions or simply to escape the world and spend time with the one you love.

Whether it's hiking to one of East Maui's spectacular waterfalls, enjoying a couples massage in a resort in Wailea, or strolling hand-in-hand along Maui's beaches, one visit to this lovely island and you'll see why falling in love comes so naturally here, perhaps more so than anywhere in the world.

Family Fun on Maui

A 750,000-gallon water tank surrounds you. As you and your family walk through the acrylic tunnel, you marvel at the manta rays and sharks swimming safely overhead. The Maui Ocean Center, voted Hawaii's top-rated family attraction by Zagat, is just one of the many family-friendly treasures you'll find on Maui.

Ride on a genuine 1890s train, known as the Sugar-Cane Train, on the Lahaina-Kaanapali Railroad. Build a sand castle at one of Maui's many beautiful beaches. Turn your 7 to 12-year-olds into Junior Rangers at the Haleakala Visitor Center. Or get your kids involved in hands-on exhibits at the Hawaii Nature Center in Wailuku.

If you're staying in a hotel or resort, they'll likely have a keiki (children's) program that includes everything from lei making to hula lessons, helping to create truly unique Maui memories to share with your children.

Haleakala National Park Maui

What: A scenic national park known as the "house of the sun"
Where: Upcountry Maui to the southeastern coast

Towering over the island of Maui and visible from just about any point, Haleakala Crater is a force of nature in every sense. At 10,023 feet above sea level, this dormant volcano is the stage for a breathtaking range of landscapes—and skyscapes. Haleakala means "house of the sun" in Hawaiian, and legend goes that the demigod Maui lassoed the sun from its journey across the sky as he stood on the volcano's summit, slowing its descent to make the day last longer.

Many visitors wake up early to drive to the Haleakala Visitor Center, the best spot to watch what may be the most spectacular sunrise on earth. As the sun peeks over the horizon, an ever-changing swirl of color and light dance across the vast sea of clouds—a sight described by Mark Twain as "the most sublime spectacle I have ever witnessed."

Perhaps just as impressive are Haleakala's sunsets and the bright, starry skies revealed at night.

Sunrises and sunsets are only two of the many reasons to pay Haleakala National Park a visit on your trip to Maui. Spanning more than 30,000 acres of public land, the stunning landscapes range from Mars-like red deserts and rock gardens near the summit to lush waterfalls and streams in the park's coastal Kipahulu section, near Hana and the beautiful Pools of Oheo.

There are numerous hiking trails that offer solitude and scenic vistas, while guided hikes and horseback rides provide an expert's insight in addition to the natural beauty. There are more endangered species here than any other park in the National Park Service, like blooming *ahinahina* (silversword) and *nene* (Hawaiian goose), the state bird. Visitors can also camp here, with separate campgrounds and cabins available.

Pools of Oheo

What: Tiered, swimmable pools located in the Oheo Gulch area of Haleakala National Park

Where: 10 miles south of Hana at mile marker 42

How much: $15 for a three-day park pass or $25 for an annual park pass. There's a $10 fee per car to enter the park

Just 15 minutes south of Hana on Highway 31 on the lower slopes of Haleakala are the famous Pools of Oheo in Oheo Gulch. Here you'll discover beautifully tiered pools fed by waterfalls. Weather permitting, you can take a dip in the tranquil waters, fed by streams starting 2 miles inland. Since Oheo is part of Haleakala National Park, the fee you pay here also admits you to the Haleakala Summit — so save your receipt!

The Kipahulu area of Haleakala National Park also boasts plenty of self-guided hiking trails that weave through forests of bamboo, past roaring cascades to the green heart of the island. Consider the Pipiwai Trail, one of the island's best trails, which leads to the 400-foot Waimoku Falls. Make sure to consult park rangers at the Kipahulu Visitor Center before you embark on this three- to five-hour hike. Expect to get muddy, and don't forget your hiking shoes.

Arrive at Haleakala National Park early – well before noon – to avoid the crowds. If you plan to watch the sunrise from the summit of Haleakala, you'll need to plan ahead because the park requires reservations for watching the sunrise (to prevent overcrowding during dark hours).

Hana Maui

What: A quiet and scenic town in East Maui

Where: The Eastern shore of Maui

Along Maui's rugged eastern coastline is the peaceful town of Hana, considered one of the last unspoiled Hawaiian frontiers. The legendary road to Hana is only 52 miles from Kahului, however the drive can take anywhere from two to four hours to complete since it's fraught with narrow one-lane bridges, hairpin turns and incredible island views.

The Hana Highway (HI-360) has 620 curves and 59 bridges. The road leads you through flourishing rainforests, flowing waterfalls, plunging pools and dramatic seascapes. There are plenty of opportunities to stop and enjoy the lovely views, so get an early start and take your time on your drive.

Historic St. Sophia's Church marks your arrival into Hana, where the pastures roll right up to the main street. The historic Travaasa Hana is a luxurious retreat in this village rooted in Hawaiian tradition. Browse the Hasegawa General Store and Hana Ranch Store for unique souvenirs. Swim and sunbathe at Hana Beach Park or Hamoa Beach, cited by author James Michener as the most beautiful beach in the Pacific. Snorkel at Waianapanapa State Park, a beautiful black sand beach. Or visit Hale Piilani, the state's largest heiau (Hawaiian temple), in Kanahu Gardens, one of five National Tropical Botanical Gardens in Hawaii.

Beyond Hana, venture 10 miles south to the outskirts of Haleakala National Park in Kipahulu. There you'll find the popular Pools of Oheo, where waterfalls spill into tiered pools leading to the sea. View these tranquil natural pools or hike up the Pipiwai Trail to the 400-foot Waimoku Falls.

Kihei

What: Sunny coastal area with 6 miles of beautiful beaches
Where: Southwest Maui, about 25 minutes from Kahului Airport

Kihei is beach-combing territory on Maui's southwest shore, the sunniest, driest end of the island. Once a regular destination for sojourning Hawaiian royalty, Kihei features 6 miles of beaches offering clear views of Kahoolawe, Molokini, Lanai and West Maui. Along with swimming and surfing, you can also find great snorkeling and kayaking — and you may even spot a giant humpback whale spouting or breaching the ocean's surface.

Kihei's Kalama Beach Park's 36 oceanfront acres are dotted with shady lawns and palm trees. The park is home to "the Cove" surf spot, beach volleyball courts, a roller-skating rink, a skate park, basketball and tennis courts, two baseball fields, picnic pavilions and a playground designed for younger kids.

A blink away are Kalpolepo, Waipuilani and the three beaches of Kamaole. Birdwatchers and nature lovers will find what they're looking for at Kealia Pond on the north end of Kihei. This National Wildlife Conservation District features endangered Hawaiian stilts and coots.

Also north of Kihei is Maalaea Bay, where pleasure boats launch to take visitors on whale watching expeditions, charter fishing excursions and snorkel trips to Molokini. Maalaea is also home to the family friendly Maui Ocean Center.

The town has a collection of affordable accommodations, with condominiums, small hotels and cottages to choose from along Kihei's beach road. You can also browse small shopping malls, a bustling farmers market and a spate of restaurants, all of which cater to residents and visitors alike. Nightlife here includes karaoke spots, dance clubs and sports bars ensuring your Kihei nights are just as fun as your days.

Maui Honeymoons

You've had your special day, so now it's time to unwind and start your life together in one of the most popular honeymoon destinations in the world. Choose from a variety of accommodations on the island, from 5 Diamond resorts to cozy beach rentals.

Then let Maui provide you both with one lasting memory after another. Drive up to Haleakala, Maui's highest peak, to see the sun rise over the clouds. Drive the road to Hana and count the waterfalls together on this scenic journey. Dine on Maui's sumptuous farm to table cuisine then stroll hand-in-hand on a moonlit night across one of Maui's serene beaches.

These are just some of the many romantic experiences Maui has to offer, so don't wait another minute. Take advantage of our honeymoon resources and start planning the vacation of your dreams.

Beaches

Beaches of Maui
With 120 miles of coastline, Maui boasts over 30 miles of beautiful beaches. On these world famous shores you'll find white, black and red sand beaches, renowned surfing and windsurfing spots as well as some of the best beaches in the world to simply swim, snorkel and sunbathe. Many are easily accessible beach parks with lifeguards, picnic facilities and restrooms. Others are undeveloped, "secret spots"

found off the beaten path. Discover Maui's world-famous beaches below.

Note: Heed all warning signs and be aware of changing conditions, strong currents and reefs. Use your own best judgment to determine whether a particular beach is appropriate for you and *your ability level.*

Makena Beach State Park (Big Beach)

What: South Maui's largest beach
Where: South of Wailea, roughly a 50-minute drive from Lahaina
More Info: Open Daily from 6 a.m.-6 p.m.

Maui's southwestern shores are home to many extraordinary beaches, including Makena Beach, also known as "Big Beach" and considered one of the island's best.

This is one of the largest beaches on Maui, with 1.5 miles of golden sand stretching as wide as 100 feet in places. Visitors can swim or snorkel in the pristine water, picnic in the shade or simply sunbathe on the seemingly endless expanse of sand.

Big Beach is located south of Wailea near the Makena Beach and Golf Resort and provides a secluded alternative to more crowded beaches in Kaanapali and Lahaina. Nestled between two black lava outcroppings, Makena offers protection from the trade winds and provides great views of the islands of Molokini and Kahoolawe. Restrooms and picnic facilities are available, and a handful of food vendors operate out of trucks both inside and just outside the park.

Note: *Always consult lifeguards before entering the water here. The shore break can be extremely dangerous, and the water is not suitable for children or inexperienced swimmers.*

Kaanapali Beach

What: West Maui's Signature beach

Where: Northwest Maui, about 50 minutes from Kahului Airport

With three miles of white sand and crystal clear water, it's no wonder why Kaanapali Beach was once named America's Best Beach. Fronting Kaanapali's hotels and resorts, this former retreat for the royalty of Maui is now a popular getaway for the world.

Kaanapali was Hawaii's first planned resort and has become a model for resorts around the globe. Five hotels and six condominium villages face this renowned beach. Also fronting Kaanapali is the open air Whalers Village, a world-class shopping complex that features a variety of exceptional shops and restaurants, a renowned whaling museum and free Hawaiian entertainment. Kaanapali also has two championship golf courses, the Royal Kaanapali and the Kaanapali Kai, where you may even see a breaching whale as you try to line up a shot.

One of Kaanapali Beach's most famous attractions is the daily cliff diving ceremony off the beach's northernmost cliffs known as Puu Kekaa, or Black Rock. Held every evening at sunset, a cliff diver lights the torches along the cliff, diving off Black Rock in a reenactment of a feat by Maui's revered King Kahekili. To soar above Kaanapali's breathtaking coastline yourself, try a zipline tour by Kaanapali Skyline Eco Adventures and enjoy a royally good view of one of Maui's signature beaches.

West Maui Beaches

Kaanapali Beach: West Maui's "signature" beach, Kaanapali Beach offers three miles of white sand. Easy walking access from all Kaanapali hotels, this was named "America's Best Beach" in 2003." Puu Kekaa, also known as Black Rock, on the northernmost section of the beach is excellent for snorkeling.

D.T. Fleming Beach Park: This classic Kapalua beach was named "America's Best Beach" in 2006. Facilities include picnic tables, restrooms and lifeguards.

Kapalua Beach: Known to Maui veterans as Old Fleming Beach, Kapalua was the first of Maui's beaches to be named "America's Best Beach" in 1991.

Launiupoko Beach Park: Just south of Lahaina, this local favorite offers a unique natural pool surrounded by a lava rock wall excellent for small children. Picnic tables and restrooms are available.

Puamana Beach County Park: This Lahaina beach provides swimming, picnic tables, restrooms, grills and a grassy park with waves that are excellent for beginning and intermediate surfers.

Central Maui Beaches

Kanaha Beach Park: World famous for its excellent windsurfing conditions, Kanaha also offers good swimming and diving. Close to Kahului, this beach is a popular spot for locals. Lifeguards, restrooms, showers and picnic tables are available.

East Maui Beaches

H.A. Baldwin Beach Park: This picture-perfect Paia beach with excellent swimming and bodysurfing. Also features a "baby beach" with a lagoon. Lifeguards, restrooms and picnic facilities are available.

Hookipa Beach Park: A world-famous contest venue for professional windsurfing. Winter surf can be massive, with excellent and safe viewing for photography. Picnic tables and restrooms are available.

Hamoa Beach: Author James Michener called Hamoa Beach the most beautiful in the Pacific. This Hana beach was named one of "America's Best Beaches" in 2006. You'll find outstanding swimming and bodysurfing as well as showers and limited facilities on this family-friendly beach.

Hana Beach Park: A favorite with local families, Hana Beach Park is one of the most popular swimming beaches on the island. Many local community events are held here.

Waianapanapa State Park: Excellent camping facilities make Waianapanapa State Park one of Maui's best beaches. You'll find a black-sand beach with good swimming, snorkeling and freshwater pools

Maui Resorts

Ask any return guest what they love most about Maui and chances are they'll tell you all about their favorite hotel or resort. Whether you prefer the plush accommodations of Wailea, the beach town of Kihei, the rustic charm of Lahaina, the Maui chic of Kaanapali or the out-of-the-way quiet of Kapalua, you'll find choices that will charm you from your first day.

Plus, Maui's resorts offer world-class amenities, from seaside spas and championship golf courses to exceptional shopping and some of Maui's most renowned restaurants.

Wailea Beach Villas, A Destination Luxury Hotel
Maui's most exclusive beachfront villa resort on famed Wailea Beach offers an indulgent vacation experience. Exquisite 2- and 3-bedroom villas are generously sized, some with its own private pool. Enjoy resort amenities and allow the Concierge to arrange a private chef or personal adventure guide.

Local Phone: (866) 384-4590

US Toll Free: (866) 384-4590

Email: drhinfo@destinationhotels.com

Courtyard Maui Kahului Airport
Courtyard By Marriott Maui Kahului Airport hotel features the latest contemporary Courtyard hotel design and exclusive amenities. Easy to use Technology with plenty of space to work or rest in our lobby. Inspiring Dining at The Bistro, and 128 relaxing guest rooms.

Local Phone: (808) 871-1800

US Toll Free: (877) 852-1880

Royal Lahaina Resort
This oceanfront Resort offers luxurious guestrooms in its 12-story tower, and garden and oceanfront cottage accommodations reminiscent of Hawaii's Plantation Era. Enjoy exceptional service, three pools, a restaurant and bars and an oceanfront Luau on the best stretch of Kaanapali Beach.

Local Phone: (808) 661-3611

US Toll Free: (808) 661-3611

Email: june.pagdilao@hawaiihotels.com

Maui Coast Hotel
Located in Sunny South Maui just across the street from a six mile stretch of Maui's beautiful and award-winning beaches, the Maui Coast Hotel is the only Premier Full Service Hotel in Kihei, one of Maui's favorite vacation destinations.

Local Phone: (808) 874-6284

US Toll Free: (800) 895-6284

Sheraton Maui Resort & Spa
Privately nestled against historic Black Rock promontory, Sheraton Maui is set amid 23 lush tropical acres on world famous Kaanapali Beach. The oceanfront resort offers 508 newly renovated guestrooms, exquisite dining, and spectacular water activities.

Local Phone: (808) 661-0031

US Toll Free: (866) 716-8109

Kaanapali Beach Hotel
Kāʻanapali Beach Hotel, fronting world-famous Kāʻanapali Beach, is officially recognized as Hawaiʻi's Most Hawaiian Hotel. Here on 11 acres of tropical gardens, our guests can relax and truly enjoy the romantic Hawaiian atmosphere. Here you will experience Aloha at its best!

Local Phone: (808) 661-0011

US Toll Free: (800) 262-8450

Andaz Maui at Wailea Resort & Spa
Seek sanctuary at a hidden gem along the coast of a world-famous island destination. Andaz Maui at Wailea radiates luxury at every turn, inviting you to revel in a unique Hawaiian cultural experience.

Local Phone: (808) 573-1234

Email: andazmauireservations@andaz.com

Residence Inn Maui Wailea
Embrace Hawaiian heritage and local culture during your stay at the new all-suites Wailea hotel. Whatever brings you to Maui, enjoy a resident-like stay with modern amenities that redefines your Hawaii experiences. Hawaii paradise living awaits.

Local Phone: (808) 891-7460

Paia Inn
The Paia Inn is located on the North Shore of Maui. Enjoy a white sandy beach with our private beach access. Each guest room offers wireless internet, flat screen TV, iPod clock radio, and complimentary coffee, tea, gym pass, daily maid service and business center.

Local Phone: (808) 579-6000
US Toll Free: (800) 721-4000
Email: info@paiainn.com

Hyatt Regency Maui Resort and Spa
Situated on 40 spectacular oceanfront acres on Ka'anapali Beach, this resort offers elegant guestrooms with private lanais and panoramic views, oceanfront spa, half-acre pool, award-winning restaurants, brand new Regency Club, and Hawaiian cultural activities, including Maui's most exciting lu'au!

Local Phone: (808) 661-1234
Email: conciergeoggrm@hyatt.com

Maui Weddings

Your special day deserves a special place and Maui provides an idyllic setting for the wedding of your dreams. Whether you're planning a casual beach wedding on the shores of West Maui or a lavish ceremony in a five-diamond resort in Wailea, Maui meets every expectation.

You'll find an impressive list of venues and resources, and expert wedding planners will attend to your every need. Nothing is spared to make sure your special day turns out exactly as you imagined. So let Maui's specialists take care of the details so you can concentrate on what matters most: each other. Learn more about Maui wedding photographers, planners and venues

Surfing on Maui

Although Waikiki and the North Shore of Oahu are legendary surf spots, Maui has its own share of famous beach to experience the "sport of kings."

To watch pro surfers in action, head to Honolua Bay and Hookipa Beach near Lower Paia during winter big wave season. East of Hookipa, you'll find Maui's most famous surf spot for big wave surfing: Peahi, also known as "Jaws." During big swells, surfers are towed into Peahi's massive waves by jet-skis. This technique has lead to the emergence of a new sport called "tow-in surfing."

For first-time surfers, Maui offers lessons at far-less intimidating surf spots in West Maui and South Maui, at beaches in Kaanapali, Lahaina and Kihei. Another option for first-timers is stand-up paddle boarding, which uses larger boards for surfers to stand upright on, using a paddle to maneuver. Maui is also famous for another form of surfing: windsurfing. Hookipa Beach on Maui's northern shore is considered the windsurfing capital of the world.

No matter which style of surfing you want to try, lessons are highly recommended for your safety and the safety of your fellow beachgoers and surfers.

Learn How to Surf on Maui

Hawaii is regarded as the birthplace of surfing, so there's no better place to try the "sport of kings." Lessons typically last 1-2 hours and are taught by experienced surfers in gentle surf breaks off of Maui's famous beaches. With a push from your instructor you're almost guaranteed to get on your feet and catch your first wave.

On the sunny northwestern side of Maui, surf schools in Lahaina will get you started and steer you away from the reef. Puamana Beach Country Park provides easy waves for beginning and intermediate surfers. Launiupoko State Park, just south of Lahaina offers easy reef waves perfect for beginners. Further south of Lahaina, the beaches of

Kihei also feature smaller waves perfect for your first ride. Many resort areas in West Maui and South Maui offer surf lessons so check with your concierge.

Maui Surfer Girls

Maui Surfer Girls ("MSG") is a co - ed surf school and overnight girls and women's surf camp. We specialize in small classes at uncrowded locations south of Lahaina. We offer 2 hour classes that include boards, booties, and rash guards. Juice and stickers available after class

Local Phone: (808) 214-0606

Email: surfschool@mauisurfergirls.com

Hawaiian Paddle Sports

Hawaiian Paddle Sports offers authentic, sustainable eco-tours that empower guests to discover a deeper appreciation of and connection to Hawaii's marine environment. Guests can choose from private kayak, outrigger canoe, canoe surfing, whale watch, and snorkel tours, or take SUP or surf lessons.

Local Phone: (808) 442-6436

Email: contact@hawaiianpaddlesports.com

Goofy Foot Surf School

Since 1994; professionally and patiently teaching surfing, safety and ocean awareness to over 40,000. Learn in 2 hours or free! Groups, private or camps available.

Local Phone: (808) 244-9283

Email: surfmaui@goofyfootsurfschool.com

Hawaiian Ocean Sports

Hawaiian Ocean Sports is one of Maui's premier ocean recreation businesses for over a decade. We offer a variety of ocean activities including surf rentals and lessons, Hawaiian outrigger cultural, turtle and snorkel tours.

Local Phone: (808) 633-2800

Email: kevinhoke@hotmail.com

Aloha Surf School

E Komo Mai, Welcome to Maui's #1 rated Surf School! Our Instructors are born and raised in Hawaii and will show you a Safe, Fun and Authentic Hawaiian Experience! Guaranteed to have you surfing in under 30 minutes or your lesson is FREE! We also offer SUP lessons and rentals. Call 808-633-2800!

Local Phone: (808) 633-2800

Email: kevinhoke@hotmail.com

Maui Surf Clinics

We focus on the complete surfing experience. Lessons are available for beginning through advanced surfers with a special emphasis on safety and ocean awareness. Group and private surf lessons as well as specialized surf clinics.

Local Phone: (808) 244-7873

Email: info@mauisurfclinics.com

Island Surfboard Rentals

Maui's Premiere Stand-up paddle board - SUP & Surfboard rentals | Free Delivery and Pick-Up | Premium Boards | Free Racks & Straps with every rental.

Local Phone: (808) 281-9835

Email: info@islandsurfboardrentals.com

Aloha Surf Clinics with Nancy Emerson Maui

Nancy Emerson started 1st surf school in Hawaii on Maui, Surfing Legend, pioneer surfing pro is the originator of "LEARN TO SURF IN ONE LESSON". Since 1973 Nancy welcomes you to a complete surfing experience, surf lessons, all levels with ocean awareness & safety, making surfing fun, safe and easy!

Local Phone: (808) 294-5544

Email: nancy@alohasurfclinicsnancyemerson.com

Snorkeling and Scuba on Maui
Explore Maui's Underwater World

Explore the unseen side of Maui on an adventure beneath the sea. Snorkel off of Maui's pristine beaches or scuba dive around Maui's most popular reefs to see colorful fish, sea turtles and coral formations. Most resort beaches along West Maui and South Maui offer opportunities for snorkelers. The northernmost part of Kaanapali Beach near Puu Kekaa (Black Rock) is known for great snorkeling.

The small, crescent shaped island of Molokini off the southwestern coast of Maui is a popular destination for snorkeling and diving. In fact, the waters and colorful reefs here are so rich with life, Molokini was named a State Marine Life and Bird Conservation District. Molokini is only accessible by boat tour. Tours are available from nearby Maalaea Harbor in Kihei and Lahaina Harbor on Maui's western shores

Pride of Maui
Pride of Maui is Maui's #1 Molokini Snorkel Tour with over 30 years experience. She is the most spacious vessel on Maui, with unsurpassed stability and amenities. Her expert crew are some of the best in the business.

Local Phone: (808) 242-0955

US Toll Free: (877) TO-PRIDE

Email: tbliss@prideofmaui.com

Four Winds II Snorkeling Adventures
Come Aboard the Maui Magic-Dolphin Discovery to explore the Kanaio Coast & Molokini or take the Four Winds II to Molokini for the longest snorkel. Enjoy our Glass Bottom Viewing Room, BBQ, Soda, Beer & Wine, and our fabulous crew all for one price!

Local Phone: (808) 879-8188

US Toll Free: (800) 736-5740

Email: info@mauiclassiccharters.com

Blue Water Rafting
Snorkel with dolphins, sea turtles, and a colorful array of tropical fish. explore the sea caves and lava arches of a hidden volcanic coastline or have a close encounter with humpback whales. Climb aboard a Blue Water Raft and let the adventure unfold.

Local Phone: (808) 879-7238

Email: info@bluewaterrafting.com

Maui Dive Shop
Maui's Leading Snorkel & Dive Center offering dive gear rentals, sales, instruction & beach wear, Maka Koa, our 48' custom dive boat, offers

dives to Molokini, Back Wall, Cathedrals, & Wreck Dives. Maka Koa offers a full breakfast & deli lunch. Free Transportation provided south & west Maui.

Local Phone: (808) 875-0333

US Toll Free: (800) 542-3483

Email: info@mauidiveshop.com

Hawaiian Ocean Sports
Hawaiian Ocean Sports is one of Maui's premier ocean recreation businesses for over a decade. We offer a variety of ocean activities including surf rentals and lessons, Hawaiian outrigger cultural, turtle and snorkel tours.

Local Phone: (808) 633-2800

Email: kevinhoke@hotmail.com

Hale Huaka'i Ocean Activity Center
Located steps away from Kā`anapali Beach Hotel's sunny shore, the new water activity center will bring Hawaiian culture to popular ocean activities such as surfing, stand up paddle boarding, snorkeling, conch shell blowing and more!

Local Phone: (808) 667-0134

US Toll Free: (800) 262-8450

Email: halehuakai@kbhmaui.com

Maui Adventure Cruises

Take the exciting Explorer Super Raft to Lanai on one of two great snorkeling adventures. First, the 4.5hr "Lanai Dolphin Adventure" includes snorkeling at 2 sites. Encounter spinner dolphins & experience Lanai's barrier reef with sea turtles and colorful tropical fish.

Local Phone: (808) 661-5550

Email: maehkyne@mauiadventurecruises.com

Sea Maui

Sea Maui is Ka'anapali's "FUN BOAT". We operate a variety of snorkel tours, dolphin and whale watching trips, Sunset Cocktail sails, private charters and more! Our 55ft catamaran pulls right up onto Ka'anapali beach for loading. Fun for the whole family!

Local Phone: (808) SEA-MAUI

Email: info@seamaui.com

Hawaii Ocean Rafting

We offer multiple whale watching tours as well as half day snorkeling adventures daily during whale season. Our high speed eco rafts are available for private charters. You can customize your own whale watch, half day, mid- day, or full day snorkeling experience.

Local Phone: (808) 661-7238

US Toll Free: (888) 677-7238

Email: islandstar@maui.net

Whale Watching on Maui

The waters surrounding Maui are the stage for some of the best whale watching in the world. Each winter (December through May), thousands of kohola (humpback whales) travel to Hawaii from colder waters to breed, calve and nurse their young. The whales are drawn to the area's shallow waters, especially the Auau Channel between Maui, Molokai and Lanai, making Maui an ideal jumping-off spot for your whale-watching voyage.

Treat yourself to scenic ocean views as expert guides take you to the best spots to observe whales playfully surfacing, tail slapping or blowing spouts in the air. Regulations prohibit boats from approaching within 100 yards of a whale, and you should never swim with or touch whales or any other marine mammals. Lahaina Harbor is home to a wide range of whale watching tours. From charter boats to passenger rafts, a stroll past the kiosks lining Lahaina Harbor reveals a variety of options during the peak of whale watching season, between January and early April. Tours are roughly 2–4 hours long.

But you don't have to go on a whale watching tour to spot whales. In fact, there are plenty of areas on Maui where humpbacks can frequently be seen from the shore during whale season. The scenic McGregor Point lookout west of Maalaea and the beaches of Kaanapali, Kihei and Wailea are also great spots to see whales.

Watch Big Wave Surfing on Maui
Perhaps not as famous as Oahu's North Shore, Maui has its own share of solid big wave surf spots. During the winter months of big wave season, Honolua Bay and Hookipa Beach in Paia are popular surf breaks. While Hookipa Beach is sandy, Honolua has a rocky shoreline so the best place to watch the surfers is from the bluffs above.

East of Hookipa is the infamous surf spot called Peahi or "Jaws." Generated by winter storms swells traveling over a barrier reef, Jaws can sometimes create 40-70 foot monster waves. To produce enough speed to surf these treacherous waves, pro tow-in surfers are literally towed-into the breaking waves by jet skis. Needless to say, leave these dangerous waves to the professionals. You can view Peahi from the cliffs above this surf spot, though space is limited.

Maui's Whaling History
From 1825 to 1860, Lahaina was the center of whaling in Hawaii. This port town was once the royal capital of the Hawaiian Kingdom before

it was moved to Honolulu in 1845. During this time, Lahaina was known as the Pacific's most significant whaling port. At its peak, whalers were hunting thousands of whales each year—to the point of near extinction. Today, conservation has helped to increase the overall whale population in Hawaii.

You can still explore Lahaina's whaling past today. Neighboring the harbor, the Pioneer Inn—which was built in 1901—recalls the ambiance of the whaling days. Echoes of the past can be found throughout this historic town, from the modest Lahaina Lighthouse (the oldest lighthouse in the Pacific) to Hale Paahao, the Old Lahaina Prison, where rowdy sailors were rounded up for the night in the 1850s. Off of Kaanapali Beach, the Whale Center of Hawaii is home to a variety of exhibits and information and is free to the public.

Heritage Sites of Maui

Heritage Sites of Hawaii are special places located throughout the islands that provide significant historical, cultural and environmental contributions to the understanding and enjoyment of Hawaii. Whether it's a unique natural wonder; a National Park or Monument; or a sacred place that encapsulates Native Hawaiian customs, beliefs and practices; these are the sites that are "must see" destinations that have been visited by the people of Hawaii for generations.

On Maui, there are two Heritage Sites of Hawaii. Haleakala National Park is a stunning natural wonder spanning from Upcountry Maui's highest point (10,023 feet) to the southeastern coast of Kipahulu. Covering 30,004 acres, this park has the largest concentration of endangered species of any National Park. It is also known for unforgettable Haleakala sunrises atop its soaring summit.

Just beyond the Maui's county seat of Wailuku, you'll discover the lush Iao Valley State Monument. Home to the Iao Needle, one of Maui's most famous landmarks, this is the site of the Battle of Kepaniwai where the forces of Kamehameha I conquered the Maui army in 1790. Culturally and spiritually significant to Maui, this beautiful Heritage Site is the perfect spot for a short, relaxing hike. Learn more about the other Heritage Sites of Hawaii.

Maui Historic Places

Maui's rich history offers plenty of special places to explore, ranging from heritage sites that provide significant historical, cultural and environmental contributions, to natural wonders, and everything in between. These must-see destinations have been visited by the people of Hawaii for generations.

Maui Heritage Sites

On Maui, there are two Heritage Sites of Hawaii. Haleakala National Park is a stunning natural wonder spanning from Upcountry Maui's highest point (10,023 feet) to the southeastern coast of Kipahulu. Covering 30,004 acres, this park has the largest concentration of endangered species of any national park. It is also known for unforgettable Haleakala sunrises atop its soaring summit.

Just beyond the Maui county seat of Wailuku, you'll discover the lush Iao Valley State Monument. Home to the Iao Needle, one of Maui's most famous landmarks, this is the site of the Battle of Kepaniwai, where the forces of King Kamehameha I conquered the Maui army in 1790. Culturally and spiritually significant to Maui, this beautiful heritage site is the perfect spot for a short, relaxing hike that's complemented by historical markers describing the battle.

Kaanapali Beach
Kaanapali was once a retreat for the royalty of Maui. On the northern side of Kaanapali Beach is the sacred spot of Puu Kekaa, also known as Black Rock. Ancient Hawaiians believed this cliff was a jumping-off place for the soul to enter the spirit world. Today, you can watch the daily sunset cliff-diving ceremony, which reenacts the feat of King Kahekili, who bravely dove from this sacred spot.

Lahaina Historic Trail

The seaport town of Lahaina served as the center of government for the Hawaiian monarchy for nearly five decades until the mid-1800s. Lahaina was also an international whaling center in the 1800s. You can visit the sites of these periods by taking the self-guided Lahaina Historic Trail, which highlights 62 important historical landmarks.

Hana

A visit to remote Hana in East Maui is like stepping back in time. Undeveloped and pristine, you can sense the tradition and aloha that surrounds this lush town. Just beyond Hana in Kipahulu, you can find the grave of famed aviator Charles Lindbergh in a small country church.

The Story of King Kamehameha I

A great warrior, diplomat and leader, King Kamehameha I united the Hawaiian Islands into one royal kingdom in 1810 after years of conflict. Kamehameha I was destined for greatness from birth. Hawaiian legend prophesized that a light in the sky with feathers like a bird would signal the birth of a great chief. Historians believe Kamehameha was born in 1758, the year Halley's comet passed over Hawaii.

Given the birth name Paiea, the future king was hidden from warring clans in secluded Waipio Valley after birth. After the death threat passed, Paiea came out of hiding and was renamed Kamehameha (The

Lonely One). Kamehameha was trained as a warrior and his legendary strength was proven when he overturned the Naha Stone, which reportedly weighed between 2.5 and 3.5 tons. You can still see the Naha Stone today in Hilo.

During this time, warfare between chiefs throughout the islands was widespread. In 1778, Captain James Cook arrived in Hawaii, dovetailing with Kamehameha's ambitions. With the help of western weapons and advisors, Kamehameha won fierce battles at Iao Valley in Maui and the Nuuanu Pali on Oahu. The fortress-like Puukohola Heiau on the island of Hawaii was built in 1790 prophesizing Kamehameha's conquest of the islands. In 1810, when King Kaumualii of Kauai agreed to become a tributary kingdom under Kamehameha, that prophecy was finally fulfilled.

Kamehameha's unification of Hawaii was significant not only because it was an incredible feat, but also because under separate rule, the Islands may have been torn apart by competing western interests. Today, four commissioned statues stand to honor King Kamehameha's memory. Every June 11th, on Kamehameha Day, each of these statues are ceremoniously draped with flower lei to celebrate Hawaii's greatest king.

Downtown Honolulu, Oahu

The most recognized Kamehameha statue stands in front of Aliiolani Hale (the judiciary building) across from Iolani Palace and a short walk from the eclectic art galleries and restaurants of Chinatown. Dedicated in 1883, this was actually the second statue created after the ship delivering the original statue from Europe was lost at sea.

Kohala, Island of Hawaii
The original statue was miraculously recovered and in 1912, the restored statue was installed near Kamehameha's birthplace at Kapaau on the island of Hawaii. Visit North Kohala to see some of Hawaii's most sacred places like Puukohola Heiau.

National Statuary Hall, Washington D.C
In 1969, the third Kamehameha statue was unveiled in the U.S. Capitol's National Statuary Hall where statues of historic figures from all 50 states are on display. A statue of Molokai's Saint Damien joins the Kamehameha I statue in this amazing collection of art.

Hilo, Island of Hawaii
Hilo was Kamehameha's first seat of government and this statue (pictured aboved), dedicated in 1997 at Wailoa State Park, is the tallest of the four statues at fourteen feet. Hilo is also home to the Naha Stone, which a young Kamehameha was said to have overturned in a feat of incredible strength. Legend said that whoever had the

strength to move the Naha Stone would rule the Hawaiian Islands. Today, the Naha Stone is located in front of the Hilo Public Library.

By Region

Central Maui

Most visitors will begin their vacations here in Central Maui, arriving at Kahului Airport. Home to much of the island's local community, Central Maui offers plenty of off-the-beaten-path treasures to uncover. Browse the small town shops and restaurants of Wailuku. Visit historic and sacred spots like Iao Valley State Park. Discover Maui's thriving arts community at galleries and performance venues like the Maui Arts & Cultural Center. Or explore the streets of Kahului for its unique variety of shops, malls and restaurants. Experience the Magic Isle like a local in Central Maui

Wailuku

What: County seat of Maui county and home to unique local businesses

Where: 10 minutes west of Kahului Airport

Just 10 minutes west from the Kahului Airport is Wailuku, a commercial center and the county seat of Maui's government. Visit

Wailuku and explore the charming wooden storefronts around Market Street, showcasing dozens of family businesses, many of which have been in continuous operation for generations. These off-the-beaten-path "Mom and Pops" are home to local favorite shops, restaurants and bakeries.

Amid these cherished establishments, a new Wailuku is also emerging, featuring contemporary boutiques, stylish cafes and laid-back coffee shops. Check out both the classic and chic during Wailuku First Friday — a fun monthly event celebrating local arts and culture. Packed with music, magicians, food, art, jewelry and fashion, this free community street party is held from 6-9 p.m., with Market Street closed to vehicular traffic from 5:30 p.m.

To find out more about this quaint town, take the "Rediscover Wailuku" walking tour developed by the Wailuku Main Street Association. The tour highlights more than 23 of the town's fascinating historical and cultural attractions, including Kaahumanu Church, the Bailey House, Pihana Kalani Heiau and the Iao Theater, built in 1927.

Nestled at the foot of the dramatic West Maui Mountains, Wailuku is also the gateway to lush Iao Valley, once a sacred burial ground for Hawaiian chiefs and home to the iconic Iao Needle

Iao Valley State Park, Maui

As of September 2016, Iao Valley State Park is closed. For the most updated details, visit the State Parks site

Towering emerald peaks guard the lush valley floor of Iao Valley State Park. Located in Central Maui just west of Wailuku, this peaceful 4,000-acre, 10-mile long park is home to one of Maui's most recognizable landmarks, the 1,200-foot Iao Needle. This iconic green-mantled rock outcropping overlooks Iao stream and is an ideal attraction for easy hiking and sightseeing.

Aside from its natural tropical beautiful, sacred Iao Valley has great historical significance. It was here in 1790 at the Battle of Kepaniwai that King Kamehameha I clashed with Maui's army in his quest to unite the islands. Even with Iao Needle serving as a lookout point, Kamehameha defeated Maui's forces in a ferocious battle that ultimately changed the course of Hawaiian history.

There is a well-marked, paved pedestrian path leading from the parking lot to view Iao Needle and the ridge-top lookout provides incredible views of the valley. The needle is sometimes covered in clouds, so an early start is your best bet for a good view. Families can also take a rainforest walk or explore interactive exhibits at the Hawaii

Nature Center, which is also located within Iao Valley. Restroom facilities are available.

East Maui

The lush, East Maui coast is famous for the winding road to Hana. Beginning in the Central Maui city of Kahului, the Hana Highway runs for 52 miles amongst waterfalls, dramatic vistas and flowering rainforests. Hana itself is a small town where Hawaiian traditions are alive and aloha is a way of life. Beyond Hana is the Kipahulu section of Haleakala National Park, the site of the beautiful Pools of Oheo. Go back in time with a day-trip through unforgettable East Maui.

Hana, Maui

Along Maui's rugged eastern coastline is the peaceful town of Hana, considered one of the last unspoiled Hawaiian frontiers. The legendary road to Hana is only 52 miles from Kahului, however the drive can take anywhere from two to four hours to complete since it's fraught with narrow one-lane bridges, hairpin turns and incredible island views.

The Hana Highway (HI-360) has 620 curves and 59 bridges. The road leads you through flourishing rainforests, flowing waterfalls, plunging pools and dramatic seascapes. There are plenty of opportunities to stop and enjoy the lovely views, so get an early start and take your time on your drive.

Historic St. Sophia's Church marks your arrival into Hana, where the pastures roll right up to the main street. The historic Travaasa Hana is a luxurious retreat in this village rooted in Hawaiian tradition. Browse the Hasegawa General Store and Hana Ranch Store for unique souvenirs. Swim and sunbathe at Hana Beach Park or Hamoa Beach, cited by author James Michener as the most beautiful beach in the Pacific. Snorkel at Waianapanapa State Park, a beautiful black sand beach. Or visit Hale Piilani, the state's largest heiau (Hawaiian temple), in Kanahu Gardens, one of five National Tropical Botanical Gardens in Hawaii.

Beyond Hana, venture 10 miles south to the outskirts of Haleakala National Park in Kipahulu. There you'll find the popular Pools of Oheo, where waterfalls spill into tiered pools leading to the sea. View these tranquil natural pools or hike up the Pipiwai Trail to the 400-foot Waimoku Falls.

Pools of Oheo, Maui

Just 15 minutes south of Hana on Highway 31 on the lower slopes of Haleakala are the famous Pools of Oheo in Oheo Gulch. Here you'll discover beautifully tiered, pools fed by waterfalls. Weather permitting, you may take a dip in these tranquil pools fed by streams starting two miles inland.

Here in the Kipahulu area of Haleakala National Park, you can explore the many self-guided hikingtrails on your own through forests of bamboo, past roaring cascades and into the green heart of the island.

Here you'll find the Pipiwai Trail, one of the best trails on the island, which leads to the 400-foot Waimoku Falls. Please consult park rangers at the Kipahulu Visitor Center before you embark on this 3 to 5 hour hike. Don't forget your hiking shoes and expect to get muddy.

South Maui

You'll find the sunniest, driest area of Maui on the peaceful southwestern coast. Blessed with miles of sandy beaches and clear views of the islands of Lanai, Molokini and Kahoolawe, South Maui is a place for lazy days and romantic nights. Explore the immersive underwater aquarium at the Maui Ocean Center in the whale-friendly Maalaea Bay. Golf at world-class courses in Wailea. Shop and dine in some of Maui's finest restaurants and resorts. Discover Maui's warm hospitality on its spectacular southern coast.

Makena Beach State Park (Big Beach)

What: South Maui's largest beach

Where: South of Wailea, roughly a 50-minute drive from Lahaina

More Info: Open Daily from 6 a.m.-6 p.m.

Maui's southwestern shores are home to many extraordinary beaches, including Makena Beach, also known as "Big Beach" and considered one of the island's best.

This is one of the largest beaches on Maui, with 1.5 miles of golden sand stretching as wide as 100 feet in places. Visitors can swim or snorkel in the pristine water, picnic in the shade or simply sunbathe on the seemingly endless expanse of sand.

Big Beach is located south of Wailea near the Makena Beach and Golf Resort and provides a secluded alternative to more crowded beaches in Kaanapali and Lahaina. Nestled between two black lava outcroppings, Makena offers protection from the trade winds and provides great views of the islands of Molokini and Kahoolawe. Restrooms and picnic facilities are available, and a handful of food vendors operate out of trucks both inside and just outside the park.

Note: *Always consult lifeguards before entering the water here. The shore break can be extremely dangerous, and the water is not suitable for children or inexperienced swimmers.*

Molokini

What: Tiny island for snorkeling and diving enthusiasts

Where: Located 3 miles off of Maui's southwestern coast

Molokini is a small, crescent moon-shaped island located just 3 miles from Maui's southwestern coast, The island stretches over 18 acres and rises 160 feet above reef-filled waters, offering visitors snorkeling and diving among a kaleidoscope of coral and more than 250 species of tropical fish.

When the United States entered World War II, the military used Molokini Crater for bombing practice. Years of protests and lobbying led the US government to deem Molokini Crater and the surrounding 77 acres a Marine Life Conservation District and Bird Sanctuary. The reef has restored its health and the fish have returned. Now the island is used primarily as a tourist destination for snorkeling and scuba diving.

Tours are available from nearby Maalaea Harbor and Lahaina. Early morning is the best time to explore this pristine reserve, and whale watching is a bonus during the winter months. If you're a scuba or snorkeling enthusiast, a visit to Molokini is a Maui must.

Wailea

What: 1,500 acres of luxurious beaches, resorts and attractions
Where: South Maui, about 35 minutes from Kahului Airport

Known for its five beautiful, crescent-shaped beaches and stellar golf courses, Wailea is a luxurious resort community in South Maui that spans 1,500 acres of land with staggering ocean views. The area exudes a sense of privacy, serenity and freedom spread across an area three times the size of Waikiki.

There are five hotels tucked into the town, including opulent resorts like the Grand Wailea Resort Hotel & Spa and the Four Seasons Resort Maui at Wailea. This resort community also includes distinctive condominiums and stately private homes.

The area's signature beaches include Wailea Beach, named "America's Best Beach" in 1999, Polo Beach, with excellent swimming and snorkeling, and Ulua Beach Park, where early morning and sunset walkers and joggers abound. The Wailea Blue, Wailea Gold and Wailea Emerald courses make up the 54 holes of championship golf that have made Wailea so famous.

Drive south about 6 miles down the coast and you'll reach Ahihi-Kinau Natural Area Reserve, which boasts a renowned snorkeling area and coastal lava field. Or continue for a couple more miles and you'll come to La Perouse Bay, where lava from Maui's last eruption flowed into the sea. The site has some nice hiking trails, including the Hoapili Trail, which winds its way along the coast through some shade and then strikes inland over the lava fields to Kanaio Beach 2 to 2.5 miles away.

Back in town, The Shops at Wailea is a destination in itself, featuring world-class restaurants and shops, along with regular entertainment programs. Wailea is also home to events such as the Maui Film Festival, February's Whale Week, as well as award-winning restaurants serving the best of Hawaii Regional Cuisine. Wailea's world-renowned spas round out an unforgettable Maui getaway.

Kihei

What: Sunny coastal area with 6 miles of beautiful beaches
Where: Southwest Maui, about 25 minutes from Kahului Airport

Kihei is beach-combing territory on Maui's southwest shore, the sunniest, driest end of the island. Once a regular destination for sojourning Hawaiian royalty, Kihei features 6 miles of beaches offering clear views of Kahoolawe, Molokini, Lanai and West Maui. Along with swimming and surfing, you can also find great snorkeling and kayaking — and you may even spot a giant humpback whale spouting or breaching the ocean's surface.

Kihei's Kalama Beach Park's 36 oceanfront acres are dotted with shady lawns and palm trees. The park is home to "the Cove" surf spot, beach volleyball courts, a roller-skating rink, a skate park, basketball and tennis courts, two baseball fields, picnic pavilions and a playground designed for younger kids.

A blink away are Kalpolepo, Waipuilani and the three beaches of Kamaole. Birdwatchers and nature lovers will find what they're looking for at Kealia Pond on the north end of Kihei. This National Wildlife Conservation District features endangered Hawaiian stilts and coots.

Also north of Kihei is Maalaea Bay, where pleasure boats launch to take visitors on whale watching expeditions, charter fishing excursions and snorkel trips to Molokini. Maalaea is also home to the family friendly Maui Ocean Center.

The town has a collection of affordable accommodations, with condominiums, small hotels and cottages to choose from along Kihei's beach road. You can also browse small shopping malls, a bustling farmers market and a spate of restaurants, all of which cater to residents and visitors alike. Nightlife here includes karaoke spots, dance clubs and sports bars ensuring your Kihei nights are just as fun as your days.

Upcountry Maui

Golden beaches give way to rolling hills and misty mountains as you ascend into Upcountry Maui, which is located on the higher elevations surrounding Haleakala — the island's highest peak. Since early times, Hawaiians have farmed the volcanic soil of Upcountry fields, growing taro and sweet potato. Today, you can take farm tours, visit a goat dairy or even sip Maui-made wines and spirits in the rustic outposts of Kula and Makawao.

Upcountry is also the stomping ground of the *paniolo*, or Hawaiian cowboys—a culture that arose in the 19th century when King Kamehameha III invited vaqueros from California to teach islanders to wrangle cattle. Further east, the 10,023-foot Haleakala presides over the "Valley Isle," with epic sunrises and otherworldly landscapes that feel more like the moon than Maui. It's a dramatic departure from the coconut palms of Kaanapali and Kapalua, but a day trip to the Upcountry will bring you closer to Maui's heartland.

Paia, Maui

What: Historic Maui town featuring Hookipa Beach, the windsurfing capital of the world
Where: About four miles east of Kahului

Just four miles into your drive to Hana from Kahului, you'll discover the historic town of Paia on Maui's north coast. Divided into Lower Paia and Paia, this hospitable community was once a booming plantation town during the heyday of Maui's sugar cane industry. Today Paia is a town of colorful, rustic storefronts filled with local art galleries, one-of-a-kind shopping boutiques and restaurants.

Grab a fish burger at the popular Paia Fishmarket, then head to Hookipa Beach, the "windsurfing capital of the world." During the winter, the big north shore waves make Hookipa Beach a magnet for pro windsurfers and kite surfers. Watch the pros compete or swim and sunbathe in the calmer summer months. Another popular Paia beach is H.A. Baldwin Beach Park, which features a baby beach with a lagoon.

Note that during the winter, wave conditions can be extremely dangerous so please heed all posted signs for your safety.

Haleakala National Park Maui

What: A scenic national park known as the "house of the sun"
Where: Upcountry Maui to the southeastern coast

Towering over the island of Maui and visible from just about any point, Haleakala Crater is a force of nature in every sense. At 10,023 feet above sea level, this dormant volcano is the stage for a breathtaking range of landscapes—and skyscapes. Haleakala means "house of the sun" in Hawaiian, and legend goes that the demigod Maui lassoed the sun from its journey across the sky as he stood on the volcano's summit, slowing its descent to make the day last longer.

Many visitors wake up early to drive to the Haleakala Visitor Center, the best spot to watch what may be the most spectacular sunrise on earth. As the sun peeks over the horizon, an ever-changing swirl of color and light dance across the vast sea of clouds—a sight described by Mark Twain as "the most sublime spectacle I have ever witnessed." Perhaps just as impressive are Haleakala's sunsets and the bright, starry skies revealed at night.

Sunrises and sunsets are only two of the many reasons to pay Haleakala National Park a visit on your trip to Maui. Spanning more than 30,000 acres of public land, the stunning landscapes range from Mars-like red deserts and rock gardens near the summit to lush waterfalls and streams in the park's coastal Kipahulu section, near Hana and the beautiful Pools of Oheo.

There are numerous hiking trails that offer solitude and scenic vistas, while guided hikes and horseback rides provide an expert's insight in addition to the natural beauty. There are more endangered species here than any other park in the National Park Service, like blooming *ahinahina* (silversword) and *nene* (Hawaiian goose), the state bird. Visitors can also camp here, with separate campgrounds and cabins available.

Stretching across Maui's southern and eastern coastline, Haleakala National Park is home to Maui's highest peak. Rising 10,023 feet above sea level, Haleakala's graceful slopes can be seen from just about any point on the island. Haleakala means "house of the sun" in Hawaiian, and legend has it that the demigod Maui lassoed the sun from its journey across the sky as he stood on the volcano's summit, slowing its descent to make the day last even longer.

The park is comprised of over 30,000 acres of public land, has three separate visitors centers and covers a range of natural environments. You can travel atop the highest peaks of Haleakala, hiking above the clouds and horseback riding across otherworldly deserts. As the park stretches out to the coast towards sea level you can even visit lush tropical areas full of waterfalls and streams.

Many visitors and locals wake up early to drive up to the Haleakala Visitor Center (9,740 feet), the best spot to watch the sunrise. On a clear morning, seeing the sunrise from the summit of Haleakala is an unforgettable experience. Even those who've witnessed the event many times say they've never seen the same sunrise twice. Perhaps just as spectacular are Haleakala's sunsets and the bright, starry skies revealed at night. Just remember, beginning February 1, 2017, the National Park Services requires a reservation for personal and rental vehicles to view the sunrise from the summit district.

The long, winding road to the summit of Haleakala takes some time to drive up, but is well worth the effort. There are numerous hiking trails that offer solitude and scenic vistas, while guided hikes provide an expert's guidance and insight. You'll discover more endangered species here than any other park in the National Park Service. You may even spot a Nene (Hawaiian goose) or a blooming ahinahina plant (silversword) on your visit. Visitors can also camp here, with two separate campgrounds and cabins available.

For more information, visit the Park Headquarters Visitor Center at 7,000 feet above sea level. The Haleakala Visitor Center is at 9,740 feet atop its summit. At sea level, the Kipahulu Visitor Center is past Hana on the southeastern coast and is near the beautiful Pools of Oheo. See why Haleakala National Park is one of Maui's most popular visitor attractions.

Kula

What: Upcountry Maui town known for its farms and botanical gardens

Where: The higher elevations of Upcountry Maui

Found in the Upcountry region of Maui, Kula is a quaint, rustic area on the slopes of Haleakala. Located in the central part of the island, Kula is also at the center of its culinary resurgence, with much of the exotic produce served at Maui's best Hawaii Regional Cuisine restaurants grown right here in the rich, volcanic soil.

The fertile fields of Kula are an ideal place to stir up your appetite by taking a farm tour. Harvest your own veggies and let the chef cook them up into a truly fresh gourmet meal at Oo Farm or walk among the sugar canes and raise a glass to sustainable farming practices at Hawaii Sea Spirits Organic Farm and Distillery, producers of OCEAN Vodka. For a more floral affair, smell the sweet lavender and marvel at the stunning views at the Alii Kula Lavender Farm or see the protea at the Shim Coffee and Protea Farm Tour. The region is also home to the Kula Botanical Gardens, filled with blooming carnations, birds of paradise and orchids.

On the way to the gardens, visitors can also see Kula's most notable landmark, the brilliant white, octagonal Holy Ghost Church. A gift from the king and queen of Portugal to the island's Portuguese plantation workers in 1894, it has been recently restored. Kula also offers the best views in Upcountry Maui, with sweeping views of Maui and the Pacific Ocean.

Makawao, Maui

What: Paniolo (Hawaiian cowboy) town and a renowned art community

Where: Upcountry Maui

Located on the mid-slopes of Maui's Haleakala volcano, Makawao has one foot in its plantation past and another in its thriving arts community. This charming town was once named one of the top 25 arts destinations in the United States.

Makawao is the biggest little town in the region locally known as Upcountry Maui and is famous for its Hawaiian cowboys, or *paniolo*. Since the late 19th century, horseback-riding paniolo have wrangled cattle in Maui's wide-open upland fields. The Makawao Rodeo, held yearly on the Fourth of July, is Hawaii's largest paniolo competition and has been an Upcountry tradition for more than 50 years. The weekend events include a parade and traditional rodeo competitions such as barrel racing, calf roping and bareback bronco riding, all with a few Hawaiian twists.

For a snack, follow the locals to get a famous cream puff from T. Komoda Store. Established in 1916 by Takezo Komoda, a Japanese plantation worker, this little store and bakery does big business. Lines can be long in the morning when everything's fresh, so come early. The bakery is closed on Wednesdays and Sundays.

You can also spend the afternoon meandering through the eclectic shops, boutiques and art galleries. It's a town of working artists, where you can watch glassblowers, wood sculptors and painters as they fulfill your order. Makawao is also home to the Hui Noeau Visual Arts Center, where visitors can take classes and explore free gallery exhibits. The combination of its paniolo heritage and its lively artistic community make Makawao a unique stop on your visit to Maui.

West Maui

The sunny northwest coast of Maui was once a retreat for Hawaiian royalty and the capitol of the Hawaiian Kingdom. Today, West Maui is home to spectacular resorts, shopping, restaurants, a wealth of activities and some of the most amazing sunsets in the world.

The Honoapiilani Highway takes you from one sun-kissed resort to the next, each with its own personality. Traveling north from Maalaea and the Maui Ocean Center, your first stop is the historic whaling town of

Lahaina. Rustic buildings recall its days as Hawaii's busiest port, while bustling shops on Front Street and winter whale watching make it a favorite port of call for cruise ship passengers.

A few minutes more on the Highway and you'll find yourself drawn into the vibrant Kaanapali Resort. Whether you're staying in the area or just passing through, a stroll on the Kaanapali Beachwalk is always in order. Families play on the beach, shoppers buzz in and out, and diners sit back and simply soak in the view.

On this side of the island, resorts melt into one another, and it doesn't take long to lead you to Kapalua, known for championship golf and private getaways. Here, the tone is a bit quieter, with understated elegance.

Despite their proximity to each other, and the other hotels nestled in between, there is one thing these resorts disagree on: which resort has the best sunset and the best view. The islands of Lanai and Molokaiare just across the channel, and as the West Maui sun sets, its rays wrap around the islands washing the coastline in a magical glow. Which sunset is the best? You'll have to find out for yourself.

Honolua Bay Maui

What: Place to watch big wave surfers during the winter
Where: Roughly a 20 minute drive north of Lahaina

Honolua Bay on Maui's northwest shore is a favorite spot for experienced surfers. During the winter high surf season, Honolua has been known to have a hollow, powerful wave that offers incredibly long rides. The bluffs above the bay offer a great vantage point for visitors to watch the pros from a safe distance.

During the calmer summer months, Honolua Bay is a popular destination for snorkeling and scuba diving. As part of the Mokuleia Marine Life Conservation District, the bay has an abundance of fish and coral formations to explore. There is only a small rocky shoreline here, so sunbathing isn't ideal.

Surfing lessons are available, but note that during the winter, wave conditions at Honolua Bay can be extremely dangerous, so for your safety please heed all posted signs and use caution.

Lahaina, Maui

What: Historic whaling village and Maui hotspot
Where: On the west side of Maui, 45 minutes from Kahului Airport

Once known as Lele, which means "relentless sun" in Hawaiian, Lahaina is a historic town that has been transformed into a Maui hotspot with dozens of art galleries and a variety of unique shops and restaurants.

Once the capital of the Hawaiian Kingdom in the early nineteenth century, Lahaina was also a historic whaling village during the whaling boom of the mid-1800s. Up to 1,500 sailors from as many as 400 ships took leave in Lahaina, including Herman Melville, who immortalized the era in his classic novel Moby Dick.

Today, Lahaina is on the National Register of Historic Places. You can still get a feel for old Lahaina as you stroll down lively Front Street, ranked one of the "Top Ten Greatest Streets" by the American Planning Association. Visit historic stops like the U.S. Seamen's Hospital, Hale Paaho (Lahaina Prison), the Pioneer Inn, Maui's oldest living banyan tree and other sites on the Lahaina Historic Trail. Approximately 55 acres of old Lahaina have been set aside as historic districts.

Immerse yourself in Maui and the Hawaiian culture by learning about the ancient mode of seafaring by canoe, take a hiking tour with local guides at Hike Maui or fall asleep to the sound of breaking waves as you camp on the beach with Camp Maui-X.

Lahaina's sunny climate and oceanfront setting also provides the perfect backdrop for a variety of activities and entertainment. Get a fresh taste of Hawaii Regional Cuisine in Lahaina's fine restaurants. Get your tickets to some of Maui's best seaside luau where you can eat, drink and watch the traditional dances of Polynesia. The award-winning show Ulalena at the Maui Theatre offers a Broadway-caliber production showcasing the culture of Hawaii.

And during the winter months, don't forget to set sail from Lahaina Harbor on an unforgettable whale watching tour. The channel off the coast of Lahaina is one of the best places in the world to spot humpback whales. Even these magnificent creatures can't get enough of Lahaina.

Kapalua Maui

What: One of Maui's premier resort areas

Where: Northwest Maui, about one hour from Kahului Airport

Kapalua, loosely translated to "arms embracing the sea," is one of Maui's premier resort areas located at the foot of the verdant Kahalawai, or West Maui mountains. Kapalua's lovely shoreline is lined with five bays and three white-sand beaches, one of which was named "The Best Beach in America" by the University of Maryland's Laboratory of Coastal Research.

In the 1800's Kapalua was known as the Honolua Ranch and then the Honolua Plantation. Today the 23,000-acre, master-planned Kapalua Resort is home to the Ritz-Carlton Kapalua, award-winning restaurants, more than 20 boutique shops, historic sites and two renowned golf courses, including the Plantation Course, home to the prestigious PGA TOUR's Tournament of Champions (January) and the Bay Course, home to the 2009 Kapalua LPGA Classic.

Host of the renowned Kapalua Wine & Food Festival (June), this spectacular area, nestled amongst Cook pines and surrounded by acres of pineapple, is the perfect getaway to indulge in the luxurious side of Maui.

Kaanapali Beach

What: West Maui's Signature beach

Where: Northwest Maui, about 50 minutes from Kahului Airport

With three miles of white sand and crystal clear water, it's no wonder why Kaanapali Beach was once named America's Best Beach. Fronting Kaanapali's hotels and resorts, this former retreat for the royalty of Maui is now a popular getaway for the world.

Kaanapali was Hawaii's first planned resort and has become a model for resorts around the globe. Five hotels and six condominium villages face this renowned beach. Also fronting Kaanapali is the open air Whalers Village, a world-class shopping complex that features a variety of exceptional shops and restaurants, a renowned whaling museum and free Hawaiian entertainment. Kaanapali also has two championship golf courses, the Royal Kaanapali and the Kaanapali Kai, where you may even see a breaching whale as you try to line up a shot.

One of Kaanapali Beach's most famous attractions is the daily cliff diving ceremony off the beach's northernmost cliffs known as Puu Kekaa, or Black Rock. Held every evening at sunset, a cliff diver lights the torches along the cliff, diving off Black Rock in a reenactment of a feat by Maui's revered King Kahekili. To soar above Kaanapali's breathtaking coastline yourself, try a zipline tour by Kaanapali Skyline Eco Adventures and enjoy a royally good view of one of Maui's signature beaches.

Food & Drink

Tried & True: Hawaii Regional Cuisine

Peter Merriman, a founding member of Hawaii Regional Cuisine (HRC) and a recipient of the James Beard Award for Best Chef: Northwest/Hawaii (along with George Mavrothalassitis of Chef Mavro

Restaurant), describes the current trend in Hawaii as a refinement, a tweaking upward, of everything from fine dining to down-home local cooking. This means sesame- or nori-crusted fresh catch on plate-lunch menus, and *huli-huli* chicken at five-diamond eateries, paired with Beaujolais and leeks and gourmet long rice.

At the same time, says Merriman, HRC, the style of cooking that put Hawaii on the international culinary map, has become watered down, a buzzword: "A lot of restaurants are paying lip service."

As it is with things au courant, it is easy to make a claim but another thing to live up to it. As Merriman points out, HRC was never solely about technique; it is equally about ingredients and the chef's creativity and integrity. "We continue to get local inspiration," says Merriman. "We've never restricted ourselves." If there is a fabulous French or Thai dish, chefs like Merriman will prepare it with local ingredients and add a creative edge that makes it distinctively Hawaiian.

HRC was established in the mid-1980s in a culinary revolution that catapulted Hawaii into the global epicurean arena. The international training, creative vigor, fresh ingredients, and cross-cultural menus of the 12 original HRC chefs have made the islands a dining destination applauded nationwide. (In a tip of the toque to island tradition, *ahi* a word ubiquitous in Hawaii has replaced *tuna* on many chic New York menus.)

Here's a sampling of what you can expect to find on a Hawaii Regional Cuisine menu: seared Hawaiian fish with *lilikoi* shrimp butter; taro-crab cakes; Pahoa corn cakes; Molokai sweet-potato or breadfruit vichyssoise; Ka'u orange sauce and Kahua Ranch lamb; fern shoots from Waipio Valley; Maui onion soup and Hawaiian bouillabaisse, with fresh snapper, Kona crab, and fresh aquacultured shrimp; blackened ahi summer rolls; herb-crusted onaga; and gourmet Waimanalo greens, picked that day. You may also encounter locally made cheeses, squash and taro risottos, Polynesian *imu*-baked foods, and guava-smoked meats. If there's pasta or risotto or rack of lamb on the menu, it could be nori (red algae) linguine with opihi (limpet) sauce, or risotto with local seafood served in taro cups, or rack of lamb in cabernet and hoisin sauce (fermented soybean, garlic, and spices). Watch for ponzu sauce, too; it's lemony and zesty, much more flavorful than the soy sauce it resembles.

Plate Lunches & More: Local Food

At the other end of the spectrum is the vast and endearing world of "local food." By that, I mean plate lunches and poke, shave ice and saimin, bento lunches and *manapua* cultural hybrids all.

Reflecting a polyglot population of many styles and ethnicities, Hawaii's idiosyncratic dining scene is eminently inclusive. Consider surfer chic: Barefoot in the sand, in a swimsuit, you chow down on a **plate lunch** ordered from a lunch wagon, consisting of fried mahimahi, "two scoops rice," macaroni salad, and a few leaves of green, typically julienned cabbage. (Generally, teriyaki beef and shoyu chicken are options.) Heavy gravy is often the condiment of choice, accompanied by a soft drink in a paper cup or straight out of the can. Like **saimin** the local version of noodles in broth topped with scrambled eggs, green onions, and sometimes pork the plate lunch is Hawaii's version of high camp.

But it was only a matter of time before the humble plate lunch became a culinary icon in Hawaii. These days, even the most chichi restaurant has a version of this modest island symbol (not at plate-lunch prices, of course), while vendors selling the real thing carb-driven meals served from wagons have queues that never end.

Because this is Hawaii, at least a few licks of poi cooked, pounded taro (the traditional Hawaiian staple crop) are a must. Other **native foods** include those from before and after Western contact, such as laulau (pork, chicken, or fish steamed in ti leaves), kalua pork (pork cooked in a Polynesian underground oven known here as an *imu*), lomi salmon (salted salmon with tomatoes and green onions), squid luau (cooked in coconut milk and taro tops), poke (cubed raw fish seasoned with onions and seaweed and the occasional sprinkling of roasted kukui nuts), haupia (creamy coconut pudding), and *kulolo* (steamed pudding of coconut, brown sugar, and taro).

Bento, another popular quick meal available throughout Hawaii, is a compact, boxed assortment of picnic fare usually consisting of neatly arranged sections of rice, pickled vegetables, and fried chicken, beef, or pork. Increasingly, however, the bento is becoming more health conscious, as in macrobiotic or vegetarian brown-rice bentos. A derivative of the modest lunch box for Japanese immigrants who once labored in the sugar and pineapple fields, bentos are dispensed everywhere, from department stores to corner delis and supermarkets.

Also from the plantations comes *manapua,* a bready, doughy sphere filled with tasty fillings of sweetened pork or sweet beans. In the old days, the Chinese "*manapua* man" would make his rounds with bamboo containers balanced on a rod over his shoulders. Today you'll find white or whole-wheat *manapua* containing chicken, vegetables, curry, and other savory fillings.

The daintier Chinese delicacy dim sum is made of translucent wrappers filled with fresh seafood, pork hash, and vegetables, served for breakfast and lunch in Chinatown restaurants. The Hong Kong-style dumplings are ordered fresh and hot from bamboo steamers rolled on carts from table to table. Much like hailing a taxi in Manhattan, you have to be quick and loud for dim sum.

For dessert or a snack, particularly on Oahu's North Shore, the prevailing choice is shave ice, Hawaii's version of a snow cone. Particularly on hot, humid days, long lines of shave-ice lovers gather for heaps of finely shaved ice topped with sweet tropical syrups. (The sweet-sour *li hing mui* flavor is a current favorite.) The fast-melting mounds, which require prompt, efficient consumption, are quite the local summer ritual for sweet tooths. Aficionados order shave ice with ice cream and sweetened adzuki beans plopped in the middle.

Ahi, Ono & Opakapaka: A Hawaiian Seafood Primer

The seafood in Hawaii has been described as the best in the world. And why not? Without a doubt, the islands' surrounding waters, including the waters of the remote northwestern Hawaiian Islands, and a growing aquaculture industry contribute to the high quality of the seafood here.

The reputable restaurants in Hawaii buy fresh fish daily at predawn auctions or from local fishermen. Some chefs even catch their ingredients themselves. "Still wiggling" and "just off the hook" are the ultimate terms for freshness in Hawaii.

Although some menus include the Western description for the fresh fish used, most often the local nomenclature is listed, turning dinner into a confusing, quasi-foreign experience for the uninitiated. To help familiarize you with the menu language of Hawaii, here's a basic glossary of Hawaii's fish:

ahi yellowfin or big-eye tuna, important for its use in sashimi and poke at sushi bars and in Hawaii Regional Cuisine

aku skipjack tuna, heavily used by local families in home cooking and poke

ehu red snapper, delicate and sumptuous, yet lesser known than opakapaka

hapuupuu grouper, a sea bass whose use is expanding

hebi spearfish, mildly flavored, and frequently featured as the "catch of the day" in upscale restaurants

kajiki Pacific blue marlin, also called *au,* with a firm flesh and high fat content that make it a plausible substitute for tuna

kumu goatfish, a luxury item on Chinese and upscale menus, served *en papillote* or steamed whole, Oriental style, with scallions, ginger, and garlic

mahimahi dolphin fish (the game fish, not the mammal) or dorado, a classic sweet, white-fleshed fish requiring vigilance among purists because it's often disguised as fresh when it's actually "fresh-frozen" a big difference

monchong bigscale or sickle pomfret, an exotic, tasty fish, scarce but gaining a higher profile on Hawaiian Island menus

nairagi striped marlin, also called *au,* good as sashimi and in poke, and often substituted for ahi in raw-fish products

onaga ruby snapper, a luxury fish, versatile, moist, and flaky

ono wahoo, firmer and drier than the snappers, often served grilled and in sandwiches

opah moonfish, rich and fatty, and versatile cooked, raw, smoked, and broiled

opakapaka pink snapper, light, flaky, and luxurious, suited for sashimi, poaching, sautéing, and baking; the best-known upscale fish

papio jack trevally, light, firm, and flavorful, and favored in Hawaiian cookery

shutome broadbill swordfish, of beeflike texture and rich flavor

tombo albacore tuna, with a high fat content, suitable for grilling

uhu parrotfish, most often encountered steamed, Chinese style

uku gray snapper of clear, pale-pink flesh, delicately flavored and moist

ulua large jack trevally, firm fleshed and versatile

Ululani's Shave Ice

David and Ululani Yamashiro are near-religious about shave ice. At their multiple shops around Maui, these shave-ice wizards take the uniquely Hawaiian dessert to new heights. It starts with the water: Pure, filtered water is frozen, shaved to feather-lightness, and patted into shape. This mini snowdrift is then doused with your choice of syrup—any three flavors from calamansi lime to lychee to red velvet cake. David makes his own gourmet syrups with local fruit purees and a dash of cane sugar.

The passionfruit is perfectly tangy, the coconut is free of cloying artificial sweetness, and the electric green kiwi is studded with real seeds. Add a "snowcap" of sweetened condensed milk, and the resulting confection tastes like the fluffiest, most flavorful ice cream ever. Locals order theirs with chewy mochi morsels, sweet adzuki beans at the bottom, or tart li hing mui powder sprinkled on top (Lahaina: 819 Front St. and 790 Front St.; Kahului: 333 Dairy Rd.; Kihei: 61 S. Kihei Rd.; and Maalaea: Maalaea General Store, 132 Maalaea Rd.; www.ululanisshaveice.com; tel. 360/606-2745; daily 10:30am–6:30pm [10:30am–10pm in Lahaina]).

Life & Language

Is Everyone Hawaiian in Hawaii?

The plantations brought so many different people to Hawaii that the state is now a rainbow of ethnic groups: Living here are Caucasians, African Americans, American Indians, Eskimos, Japanese, Chinese, Filipinos, Koreans, Tahitians, Vietnamese, Hawaiians, Samoans, Tongans, and other Asian and Pacific Islanders. Add a few Canadians, Dutch, English, French, Germans, Irish, Italians, Portuguese, Scottish, Puerto Ricans, and Spaniards. Everyone's a minority here.

In combination, it's a remarkable potpourri. Many people retain an element of the traditions of their homeland. Some Japanese Americans in Hawaii, generations removed from the homeland, are more traditional than the Japanese of Tokyo. And the same is true of many Chinese, Koreans, Filipinos, and others, making Hawaii a kind of living museum of various Asian and Pacific cultures.

Do You Have to Speak Hawaiian in Hawaii?

Almost everyone here speaks English. But many folks in Hawaii now speak Hawaiian as well. All visitors will hear the words *aloha* and *mahalo* (thank you). If you've just arrived, you're a *malihini*. Someone who's been here a long time is a *kamaaina*. When you finish a job or your meal, you are *pau* (finished). On Friday it's *pau hana,* work finished. You eat *pupu* (Hawaii's version of hors d'oeuvres) when you go *pau hana*.

The Hawaiian alphabet, created by the New England missionaries, has only 12 letters: the five regular vowels (*a, e, i, o,* and *u*) and seven consonants (*h, k, l, m, n, p,* and *w*). The vowels are pronounced in the Roman fashion: that is, *ah, ay, ee, oh,* and *oo* (as in "too") not *ay, ee, eye, oh,* and *you,* as in English. For example, *huhu* is pronounced *who-who*. Most vowels are sounded separately, though some are pronounced together, as in Kalakaua: Kah-lah-*cow*-ah.

Following are some basic Hawaiian words that you'll often hear in Hawaii.

| **alii** Hawaiian royalty | **lomilomi** massage |

aloha greeting or farewell	**mahalo** thank you
halau school	**makai** a direction, toward the sea
hale house or building	**mana** spirit power
heiau Hawaiian temple or place of worship	**mauka** a direction, toward the mountains
kahuna priest or expert	**muumuu** loose-fitting gown or dress
kamaaina old-timer	**ono** delicious
kapa tapa, bark cloth	**pali** cliff
kapu taboo, forbidden	**paniolo** Hawaiian cowboy(s)
keiki child	**wiki** quick
kupuna respected elder	**Pidgin: 'Eh Fo' Real, Brah**
lanai porch or veranda	

If you venture beyond the tourist areas, you might hear another local tongue: pidgin English, a conglomeration of slang and words from the Hawaiian language. "Broke da mouth" (tastes really good) is the favorite pidgin phrase and one you might hear; "'Eh fo' real, brah" means "It's true, brother." You could be invited to hear an elder "talk story" (relating myths and memories). But because pidgin is really the province of the locals, your visit to Hawaii is likely to pass without your hearing much pidgin at all.

Restaurants

Where to Eat on Maui

When it comes to dining in Maui, all I can say is: Come hungry and bring your wallet. Dining has never been better on the Valley Isle, which is presently producing numerous enterprising and imaginative chefs. The farm-to-table concept has finally taken root on this bountiful island where, in past years, up to 90 percent of the food has been imported. Today, chefs and farmers collaborate on menus, filling plates with tender micro-greens and heirloom tomatoes picked that morning. Fishers reel in glistening opakapaka (pink snapper), and ranchers offer up flavorful cuts of Maui-grown beef.

A new crop of inspired chefs is taking these ripe ingredients to new heights. At Ka'ana Kitchen, chef Isaac Bancaco is outshining his celebrity neighbor, "Iron Chef" Masaharu Morimoto (who recently brought his high-octane Japanese fusion cuisine to Wailea). Both are outstanding; make time for each. Next door at Migrant, "Top Chef" finalist Sheldon Simeon is showcasing gourmet local-style dishes with Filipino accents. Up the street, chefs Brian Etheredge and Chris Kulis are making traditional Italian seem brand-new again at Capische.

The pioneers of Hawaii Regional Cuisine are still stirring things up in the kitchen as well. Alan Wong recently opened Amasia at the Grand Wailea; Peter Merriman opened a location in Kapalua with gasp-inducing views; and Mark Ellman of Mala Ocean Tavern, added Honu and Migrant to his empire.

Stellar dining experiences all, but expect to pay for them. Still, you don't have to spend a fortune to eat well on Maui. Although the old-fashioned, multigenerational mom-and-pop diners are disappearing, eclipsed by the sophisticated newcomers, Maui does have a few budget eateries, noted below. But if you want to feast, there's never been a better time to do so on Maui.

Central Maui

The Queen Kaahumanu Center, the structure that looks like a white "Star Wars" umbrella in the center of Kahului, at 275 Kaahumanu Ave. (10 min. from Kahului Airport on Hwy. 32), has a popular food court. Eateries include Ramen Ya, for a steaming bowl of noodles, and Maui Tacos. Outside the food court, but still in the shopping center, is Ruby's, a kid-friendly '50s-style diner dishing out burgers, fries, and shakes. When you leave Kaahumanu Center, take a moment to gaze at the West Maui Mountains to your left from the parking lot.

Nightlife

Maui Nightlife

Maui tends to turn out the lights at 10pm; nightlife options on this island are limited, but you'll find a few gems listed below.

The island's most prestigious entertainment venue is the $32-million Maui Arts & Cultural Center, in Kahului (www.mauiarts.org; tel. 808/242-7469). The center is as precious to Maui as the Met is to New York, with a visual-arts gallery, an outdoor amphitheater, offices, rehearsal space, a 300-seat theater for experimental performances, and a 1,200-seat main theater. Check the website for schedules and buy your tickets in advance.

Hawaiian Music--The best of Hawaiian music can be heard every Wednesday night at the Napili Kai Beach Resort's indoor amphitheater, thanks to the Masters of Hawaiian Slack Key Guitar Series (www.slackkey.com; tel. 888/669-3858). The weekly shows present a side of Hawaii that few visitors ever get to see. Host George Kahumoku, Jr., introduces a new slack key master every week. Not only is there incredible Hawaiian music and singing, but George and his guest also "talk story" about old Hawaii, music, and Hawaiian culture. Not to be missed.

The major hotels generally have lobby lounges offering Hawaiian music, soft jazz, or hula shows beginning at sunset. If Hapa, Amy Hanaialii, or Keali'i Reichel are playing anywhere on their native island, don't miss them; they're among the finest Hawaiian musicians around today. Willie K (Maui's answer to Jimi Hendrix) performs weekly at Mulligan's on the Blue, 100 Kaukahi St., Wailea (www.mulligansontheblue.com; tel. 808/874-1131).

West Maui

Make time to see 'Ulalena , Maui Theatre, 878 Front St., Lahaina (www.ulalena.com; tel. 808/856-7900), a "Cirque du Soleil"–style entertainment that weaves Hawaiian mythology with drama, dance, and state-of-the-art multimedia capabilities in a multimillion-dollar theater. It's interactive; dancers stream down the aisles and musicians play from surprising corners. The story unfolds seamlessly; at the end, you'll be shocked to realize that not a single word of dialogue was spoken. Performances are given Tuesday through Saturday. Tickets are $60 to $80 for adults, $30 to $50 for children 6 to 12.

A very different type of live entertainment, Warren & Annabelle's, 900 Front St., Lahaina (www.warrenandannabelles.com; tel. 808/667-6244), is a magic/comedy cocktail show with illusionist Warren Gibson and "Annabelle," a ghost from the 1800s who plays the grand piano (even taking requests from the audience) as Warren dazzles you with his sleight-of-hand magic. Appetizers, desserts, and cocktails are available (either as a package or a la carte). Check-in is at 5 and 7:30pm. The show-only price is $64; the show plus gourmet appetizers and dessert costs $105. You must be 21 to attend.

You won't have to ask what's going on at Cheeseburger in Paradise, 811 Front St., Lahaina (www.cheeseburgerland.com; tel. 808/661-4855), the two-story green-and-white building at the corner of Front and Lahainaluna streets. Just go outside and you'll hear it. Loud, live, and lively tropical rock blasts into the streets and out to sea nightly from 4:30 to 10pm.

Other venues for music in west Maui include the following:

- Hula Grill, in Whalers Village, Kaanapali (tel. 808/667-6636), has live music (usually Hawaiian) every day from 11am to 9pm.

- Kimo's, 845 Front St., Lahaina (tel. 808/661-4811), has live musicians every night at various times; call for details.

- Pioneer Inn, 658 Wharf St., Lahaina (tel. 808/661-3636), offers a variety of live music Tuesday through Thursday nights 5:30 to 8pm.

- Sansei Seafood Restaurant & Sushi Bar, 600 Office Rd., Kapalua (tel. 808/669-6286), has karaoke on Thursday through Saturday from 10pm to 1am.

- Sea House Restaurant, at the Napili Kai Beach Resort, Napili (tel. 808/669-1500), has live music nightly from 7 to 9pm.

South Maui

- The Kihei, Wailea, and Maalaea areas in south Maui also feature music in a variety of locations:

- Kahale's Beach Club, 36 Keala Place, Kihei (tel. 808/875-7711), is a bit of a dive bar, but has a potpourri of rock music nightly.

- Life's a Beach, 1913 S. Kihei Rd., Kihei (www.mauibars.com; tel. 808/891-8010), has live music nightly and karaoke; call for times.

- Mulligan's on the Blue, 100 Kaukahi St., Wailea (www.mulligansontheblue.com; tel. 808/874-1131), offers rollicking Irish music on Sunday, a Wednesday dinner show with local legend Willie K, and other entertainers during the week.

- Sansei Seafood Restaurant & Sushi Bar, in Kihei Town Center, 1881 South Kihei Rd., Kihei (www.sanseihawaii.com; tel. 808/879-0004), has karaoke Thursday through Saturday from 10pm to 1am.

➢ South Shore Tiki Lounge, 1913 S. Kihei Rd., Kihei (www.southshoretikilounge.com; tel. 808/874-6444), has dancing nightly from 10pm to 1:30am.

luau, Maui Style

Most of the larger hotels in Maui's major resorts offer luau on a regular basis. You'll pay about $80 to $120 to attend one, but don't expect it to be a homegrown affair prepared in the traditional Hawaiian way. There are, however, commercial luau that capture the romance and spirit of the luau with quality food and entertainment.

Maui's best choice is indisputably the nightly Old Lahaina Luau (www.oldlahainaluau.com; tel. 800/248-5828 or 808/667-1998). Located just ocean-side of the Lahaina Cannery, the Old Lahaina Luau maintains its high standards in food and entertainment—and enjoys an oceanfront setting that is peerless. Local craftspeople display their wares only a few feet from the ocean. Seating is provided on lauhala mats for those who wish to dine as the traditional Hawaiians did, but there are tables for everyone else. There's no fire dancing in the program, but you won't miss it. This luau offers a healthy balance of entertainment, showmanship, authentic high-quality food, educational value, and sheer romantic beauty. (No watered-down mai tais, either; these are the real thing.)

The luau begins at sunset and features Tahitian and Hawaiian entertainment, including ancient hula, hula from the missionary era, modern hula, and an intelligent narrative on the dance's rocky course of survival into modern times. The food, served from an open-air thatched structure, is as much Pacific Rim as authentically Hawaiian: imu-roasted kalua pig, baked mahimahi in Maui onion cream sauce, guava chicken, teriyaki sirloin steak, lomi salmon, poi, dried fish, poke, Hawaiian sweet potato, sautéed vegetables, seafood salad, and taro leaves with coconut milk. The cost is $109 for adults, $78 for children 12 and under.

For information on all of Maui's luaus, go to www.mauihawaiiluau.com.

Upcountry Maui
Upcountry in Makawao, the party never ends at Casanova, 1188 Makawao Ave. (www.casanovamakawao.com; tel. 808/572-0220), the popular Italian ristorante. If a big-name Mainland band is resting up on Maui following a sold-out concert on Oahu, you may find its members setting up for an impromptu night here. DJs take over on Wednesday (ladies' night); on Friday and Saturday, live music starts between 9 and 10pm and continues to 1:30am. Expect blues, rock 'n' roll, reggae, jazz, and Hawaiian. Elvin Bishop, the local duo Hapa, Los Lobos, and others have taken Casanova's stage. The cover is usually $10 to $20.

Paia & Central Maui

In Central Maui, The Kahului Ale House, 355 E. Kamehameha Ave., Kahului (www.alehouse.net; tel. 808/877-9001), features live music or a DJ most nights; call for schedule.

In Paia, Charley's Restaurant, 142 Hana Hwy. (www.charleysmaui.com; tel. 808/579-8085), features an eclectic selection of music, from country-western to reggae to rock 'n' roll Thursday through Saturday.

The Entertainment Scene

Centered around the $32-million Maui Arts & Cultural Center (MACC), in Kahului (tel. 808/242-7469; www.mauiarts.org), the performing arts are alive and well on this island. The MACC remains the island's most prestigious entertainment venue, a first-class center for the visual and performing arts. Bonnie Raitt has performed here, as have Hiroshima, Pearl Jam, Ziggy Marley, Tony Bennett, the American Indian Dance Theatre, the Maui Symphony Orchestra, and Jonny Lang, not to mention the finest in local talent. The center boasts a visual-arts gallery, an outdoor amphitheater, offices, rehearsal space, a 300-seat theater for experimental performances, and a 1,200-seat main theater. The center's activities are well publicized locally, so check the *Maui News* or ask your hotel concierge what's going on during your visit.

In Search of Hawaiian, Jawaiian & More

Nightlife options on Maui are limited-there are very few clubs on the island; most clubs and bars with entertainment or dancing tend to be located close to resort areas. Since Maui is so spread out, you may find yourself driving a great distance to get to a club that is providing the kind of entertainment you want. Here's a tip: first check out the night life and entertainment options in the major hotels near you. Hotels generally have lobby lounges offering Hawaiian music, soft jazz, or hula shows beginning at sunset. Other music venues are listed.

The best of Hawaiian music can be heard every Wednesday night at 7:30pm at the Napili Kai Beach Resort's indoor amphitheater, thanks to the Grammy-winning Masters of Hawaiian Slack Key Guitar Concert Series (tel. 888/669-3858;www.slackkey.com). The weekly shows present a side of Hawaii that few visitors ever get to see. Host George Kahumoku, Jr., introduces a new slack-key master every week. Not only is there incredible Hawaiian music and singing, but George and his guest also "talk story" about old Hawaii, music, and Hawaiian culture. Not to be missed.

At the Movies

The 12-screen movie megaplex at the Maui Mall, 70 E. Kaahumanu Ave. (tel. 808/249-2222), in Kahului, features current releases. In June, the not-to-be-missed Maui Film Festival ★★★ (tel. 808/572-3456 or 579-9244; www.mauifilmfestival.com) puts on nights of cinema under the stars in Wailea. The Maui Film Festival also presents "Academy House" films for the avant-garde, ultrahip movie buff Wednesday nights at the Maui Arts & Cultural Center, 1 Cameron Way (just off Kahului Beach Rd.), Kahului, usually followed by local catering (with bar) and live music and poetry readings.

Film buffs can check the local newspapers to see what's playing at the other theaters around the island: the Kaahumanu Theatres, at the Kaahumanu Center, in Kahului (tel. 808/873-3137); the Kukui Mall Theater, 1819 S. Kihei Rd., in Kihei (tel. 808/874-8624); the Wallace Theaters at the Wharf Cinema Center, 658 Front St., in Lahaina (tel. 808/249-2222); and the Front Street Theatres at the Lahaina Center, 900 Front St. (tel. 808/249-2222).

The Best Place in the World to See a Movie Imagine lounging on a comfy beach chair on the island of Maui watching the stars come out in the night sky. As soon as it gets dark enough, the biggest outdoor screen you've ever seen comes to life with a film premiere. This has to be the best place in the entire world to watch movies.

If you're headed to Maui in June, plan your travel dates around the Maui Film Festival (tel. 808/572-3456 or 579-9244;

www.mauifilmfestival.com), which always starts the Wednesday before Father's Day. This is an event you won't want to miss. The 5-day festival features nightly films in the "Celestial Cinema," an under-the-stars, open-air "outdoor theater" on the Wailea Golf Course. The event features premieres and special advance screenings on a 50-foot-wide screen in Dolby Digital Surround Sound. Festival organizer and film producer Barry Rivers selects "life-affirming" films that often become box-office hits.

In addition to the 5 days and nights of films and filmmaker panels, there are many other events: a Taste of Chocolate night, a Taste of Wailea (with Maui's top chefs creating exquisite culinary masterpieces), a Starry Night dance party, and a host of other foodie events. For the family, there's a Father's Day concert of contemporary Hawaiian music, a sand-sculpture contest, and picnics. And for those interested in Hawaii culture, the festival presents TheStarShow, where live images of celestial objects are projected onto the screen, as experts in Polynesian astronomy and cultural history take the audience on a tour of the night sky and Polynesian navigational lore.

As Rivers puts it, "rising stars, shooting stars, movie stars, all under the stars."

At the Theater

It's not Broadway, but Maui does have live community theater at the Iao Theater, 68 N. Market St., in Wailuku (tel. 808/242-6969 for the box office and program information or 808/244-8680 for the dinner theater options; www.mauionstage.com). Shows range from locally written productions to well-known plays and musicals.

Shopping

Maui Shopping

Maui's best shopping is found in the small, independent boutiques and galleries scattered around the island—particularly in Makawao and Paia. (If you're in the market for a bikini, there's no better spot than the intersection of Baldwin Ave. and Hana Hwy. on Maui's north shore.) The two upscale resort shopping malls, the Shops at Wailea in South Maui and Whalers Village in Kaanapali, have everything from Louis Vuitton and Coach to Gap—plus a handful of local designers to boot. If you're looking for that perfect souvenir, consider visiting one of Maui's farms (or farmers' markets), most of which offer fantastic value-added products. Take home Kaanapali coffee, Kula lavender spice rub, Maui Ocean vodka, Maui Gold pineapple, and other tasty treats that can be shipped worldwide.

Central Maui
Kahului

Kahului's shopping is concentrated in two malls. The Maui Mall, 70 E. Kaahumanu Ave. (www.mauimall.com; tel. 808/877-8952), is the place of everyday retail, from Longs Drugs and Whole Foods to Tasaka Guri Guri (the decades-old purveyor of inimitable icy treats that are neither ice cream nor shave ice, but something in between) and Kahului's largest movie theater, a 12-screen megaplex that features mainly current releases.

Queen Kaahumanu Center, 275 Kaahumanu Ave. (www.queenkaahumanucenter.com; tel. 808/877-3369), a 10-minute drive from the Kahului Airport, offers two levels of shops, restaurants, and theaters. It covers the bases, from arts and crafts to a Foodland and everything in between: a thriving food court; the island's best beauty supply, Lisa's Beauty Supply & Salon (tel. 808/877-6463) and its sister store for cosmetics, Madison Avenue Day Spa and Boutique(tel. 808/873-0880); mall standards like Macy's, Sears, Sunglass Hut, and Local Motion (surf and beach wear).

Wailuku

Wailuku's vintage architecture, antiques shops, and mom-and-pop eateries imbue the town with charm. You won't find any plastic aloha in Wailuku; in fact, this is the best place to buy authentic Hawaiian souvenirs.

Central Maui Edibles

Maui's produce has long been a source of pride for islanders. You'll find a selection of fresh Maui-grown fruit, vegetables, flowers, and plants at the Ohana Farmers Market, at Queen Kaahumanu Shopping Center (tel. 808/877-3369), every Tuesday, Wednesday, and Friday from 8am to 4pm.

In the northern section of Wailuku, Takamiya Market, 359 N. Market St. (tel. 808/244-3404), is much loved by local folks and visitors with adventurous palates, who often drive all the way from Kihei to stock up on picnic fare and mouthwatering ethnic foods for sunset gatherings. Unpretentious home-cooked foods from East and West are prepared daily and served on plastic-foam plates. The chilled-fish counter has fresh sashimi and poke, and prepared foods include mounds of shoyu chicken, fried squid, kalua pork, Chinese noodles, fiddlehead ferns, and Western comfort foods such as cornbread and potato salad.

West Maui

Lahaina

Lahaina's merchants and art galleries go all out from 7 to 10pm every Friday, when Art Night brings an extra measure of hospitality and community spirit. The Art Night openings are usually marked with live entertainment and refreshments, plus a livelier-than-usual street scene. If you're in Lahaina on the second or last Thursday of the month, stroll by the front lawn of the Baldwin Home Museum, 120 Dickenson St. (at Front St.), for a splendid look at the craft of lei-making (you can even buy the results).

Across from the seawall on Front Street, you'll find the Outlets of Maui, 900 Front St. (www.theoutletsofmaui.com; tel. 808/667-9216). There's plenty of free validated parking and easy access to more than 2 dozen outlet shops including Calvin Klein, Coach, Banana Republic, Adidas, Kay Jewelers, and more. Ruth's Chris Steak House serves its famed cuts of beef here, and the Hard Rock Cafe serves lunch and dinner with live music most nights.

At the northern end of Lahaina town, what was formerly a big, belching pineapple cannery is now a maze of shops and restaurants known as the Lahaina Cannery Mall, 1221 Honoapiilani Hwy. (www.lahainacannerymall.com; tel. 808/661-5304). Inside the air-conditioned building there's a Longs Drugs and a 24-hour Safeway for groceries. Footprints Maui may surprise you with its shoe selection—everything from Cole Haan sophisticates to inexpensive sandals. In the food court, try Ba-Le FrenchSandwich and Bakery for great banh mi and croissant sandwiches, while L & L Drive-Inn sells plate lunches. At

Lulu's Lahaina Surf Club & Grill, you can get a frosty beer and watch big-wave surfers on the multiple flatscreen TVs.

Honokowai, Kahana & Napili

Those driving north of Kaanapali toward Kapalua will notice the HonokowaiMarketplace, on Lower Honoapiilani Road, only minutes before the Kapalua Airport. It houses restaurants and coffee shops, a dry cleaner, the flagship TimesSupermarket, and a few clothing stores.

South Maui

Kihei

Kihei is one long strip of strip malls. Most of the shopping here is concentrated in the Azeka Place Shopping Center on South Kihei Road. Across the street, Azeka Place II houses several prominent attractions, including a cluster of specialty shops with everything from children's clothes to shoes, sunglasses, and swimwear.

Fresh Flowers in Kula

Like anthuriums on the Big Island, proteas are a Maui trademark and an abundant crop on Haleakala's rich volcanic slopes. They also travel well, dry beautifully, and can be shipped worldwide with ease. Proteas of Hawaii, 15200 Haleakala Hwy., Kula (www.proteasofhawaii.com; tel. 808/878-2533, ext. 210), located next door to the Kula Lodge, is a reliable source of this exotic flower.

Upcountry Edibles

Working folks in Makawao pick up spaghetti and lasagna, sandwiches, salads, and changing specials from the Rodeo General Store, 3661 Baldwin Ave. (tel. 808/572-1868). At the back of the store, a superior wine selection is housed in its own temperature-controlled cave.

For just shy of a century, the hard-working Komoda family has been satisfying Maui's sweet tooth. Untold numbers have creaked over the wooden floors to pick up a box of famous cream puffs at T. Komoda Store and Bakery, 3674 Baldwin Ave. (tel. 808/572-7261). The coveted pastries (filled with vanilla or mocha cream) are just the beginning; stick donuts encrusted with macadamia nuts, Chantilly cakes, fruit pies, and butter rolls keep loyal customers coming to this nostalgic piece of Maui history. Old-timers know to arrive before noon or miss out. Bring cash and be aware of the odd business hours: It's open 7am to 5pm on Monday, Tuesday, Thursday, and Friday, and 7am to 2pm on Saturday.

East Maui

Paia has no fewer than five boutiques dedicated to Maui's sun-kissed beach uniform, the bikini. And that's not all; many of the other shops lining Baldwin Avenue and Hana Highway also sell swimwear. Head to this north-shore beach town for everything from skimpy Brazilian bikinis to full-figured, mix-and-match-your-own suits. The best of the bunch are Maui Girl, 12 Baldwin Ave. (www.maui-girl.com; tel. 808/579-9266; daily 9am–6pm), a cheery beach shack that has outfitted more than one "Sports Illustrated" cover model; and Le Tarte, 24 Baldwin Ave. (www.letarteswimwear.com; tel. 808/579-6022; daily 10am–6pm), an ultra-chic boutique with embroidered beach cover-ups so pretty you'll want to wear them out and about. Maui Girl and Le Tarte are both owned by local designers, as are two other great spots to shop for suits: Wings Hawaii, 69 Hana Hwy. (www.wingshawaii.com; tel. 808/579-3110), and Tamara Catz, 83 Hana Hwy. (www.tamaracatz.com; tel. 808/579-9184).

Environment

The first Hawaiian islands were born of violent volcanic eruptions that took place deep beneath the ocean's surface about 70 million years ago more than 200 million years after the major continental landmasses were formed. As soon as the islands emerged, Mother Nature's fury began to carve beauty from barren rock. Untiring volcanoes spewed forth rivers of fire that cooled into stone. Severe tropical storms, some with hurricane-force winds, battered and blasted the cooling lava rock into a series of shapes. Ferocious earthquakes flattened, shattered, and reshaped the islands into precipitous valleys, jagged cliffs, and recumbent flatlands. Monstrous surf and gigantic tidal waves rearranged and polished the lands above and below the reaches of the tide.

It took millions of years for nature to shape the familiar form of Diamond Head on Oahu, Maui's majestic peak of Haleakala, the waterfalls of Molokai's northern side, the reefs of Hulopoe Bay on Lanai, and the lush rainforests of the Big Island. The result is an island chain like no other a tropical dreamscape of a landscape rich in flora and fauna, surrounded by a vibrant underwater world.

The Flora of the Islands

Hawaii is filled with sweet-smelling flowers, lush vegetation, and exotic plant life.

African Tulip Trees Even from afar, you can see the flaming red flowers on these large trees, which can grow to be more than 50 feet tall. The buds hold water, and Hawaiian children use the flowers as water pistols.

Angel's Trumpets These small trees can grow up to 20 feet tall, with an abundance of large (up to 10-in. diameter) pendants white or pink flowers that resemble, well, trumpets. The Hawaiians call them *nana-honua,* which means "earth gazing." The flowers, which bloom continually from early spring to late fall, have a musky scent. Warning: All parts of the plant are poisonous and contain a strong narcotic.

Anthuriums Anthuriums originally came from the tropical Americas and the Caribbean islands. There are more than 550 species, but the most popular are the heart-shaped red, orange, pink, white, and purple flowers with tail-like spathes. Look for the heart-shaped green leaves in shaded areas. These exotic plants have no scent but will last several weeks as cut flowers. Anthuriums are particularly prevalent on the Big Island.

Banyan Trees Among the world's largest trees, banyans have branches that grow out and away from the trunk, forming descending roots that grow down to the ground to feed and form additional trunks, making the tree very stable during tropical storms. The banyan in the courtyard next to the old courthouse in Lahaina, Maui, is an excellent example of a spreading banyan it covers 2/3 acre.

Birds of Paradise These natives of Africa have become something of a trademark of Hawaii. They're easily recognizable by the orange and blue flowers nestled in gray-green bracts, looking somewhat like birds in flight.

Bougainvillea Originally from Brazil, these vines feature colorful, tissue-thin bracts, ranging in color from majestic purple to fiery orange, that hide tiny white flowers.

Breadfruit Trees A large tree more than 60 feet tall with broad, sculpted, dark-green leaves, the famous breadfruit produces a round, head-size green fruit that's a staple in the diets of all Polynesians. When roasted or baked, the whitish-yellow meat tastes somewhat like a sweet potato.

Bromeliads There are more than 1,400 species of bromeliads, of which the pineapple plant is the best known. "Bromes," as they're affectionately called, are generally spiky plants ranging in size from a few inches to several feet in diameter. They're popular not only for their unusual foliage, but also for their strange and wonderful flowers. Used widely in landscaping and interior decoration, especially in resort areas, bromeliads are found on every island.

Coffee Hawaii is the only state that produces coffee commercially. Coffee is an evergreen shrub with shiny, waxy, dark-green pointed leaves. The flower is a small, fragrant white blossom that develops into 1/2-inch berries that turn bright red when ripe. Look for coffee at elevations above 1,500 feet on the Kona side of the Big Island and on large coffee plantations on Kauai, Molokai, Oahu, and Maui.

Ginger White and yellow ginger flowers are perhaps the most fragrant in Hawaii. Usually found in clumps growing 4 to 7 feet tall in areas blessed by rain, these sweet-smelling, 3-inch-wide flowers are composed of three dainty petal-like stamens and three long, thin petals. Ginger was introduced to Hawaii in the 19th century from the Indonesia-Malaysia area. Look for white and yellow ginger from late spring to fall. If you see ginger on the side of the road, stop and pick a few blossoms your car will be filled with a divine fragrance the rest of the day.

Other members of the ginger family frequently seen in Hawaii include red, shell, and torch ginger. Red ginger consists of tall green stalks with foot-long red "flower heads." The red "petals" are actually bracts, which protect the 1-inch-long white flowers. Red ginger, which does not share the heavenly smell of white ginger, lasts a week or longer when cut. Look for red ginger from spring through late fall. Shell ginger, which originated in India and Burma, thrives in cool, wet mountain forests. These plants, with their pearly white, clamshell-like blossoms, bloom from spring to fall.

Perhaps the most exotic ginger is the red or pink torch ginger. Cultivated in Malaysia as seasoning, torch ginger rises directly out of the ground. The flower stalks, which are about 5 to 8 inches in length, resemble the fire of a lighted torch. This is one of the few types of ginger that can bloom year-round.

Heliconia Some 80 species of the colorful heliconia family came to Hawaii from the Caribbean and Central and South America. The bright yellow, red, green, and orange bracts overlap and appear to unfold like origami birds. The most obvious heliconia to spot is the lobster claw, which resembles a string of boiled crustacean pincers. Another prolific heliconia is the parrot's beak: Growing to about hip height, it's composed of bright-orange flower bracts with black tips. Look for parrot's beaks in spring and summer.

Hibiscus The 4- to 6-inch hibiscus flowers bloom year-round and come in a range of colors, from lily white to lipstick red. The flowers resemble crepe paper, with stamens and pistils protruding spirelike from the center. Hibiscus hedges can grow up to 15 feet tall. The yellow hibiscus is Hawaii's official state flower.

Jacaranda Beginning around March and sometimes lasting until early May, these huge lacy-leaved trees metamorphose into large clusters of spectacular lavender-blue sprays. The bell-shaped flowers drop quickly, leaving a majestic purple carpet beneath the tree.

Macadamia A transplant from Australia, macadamia nuts have become a commercial crop in recent decades in Hawaii, especially on the Big Island and Maui. The large trees up to 60 feet tall bear a hard-shelled nut encased in a leathery husk, which splits open and dries when the nut is ripe.

Monkeypod Trees The monkeypod is one of Hawaii's most majestic trees; it grows more than 80 feet tall and 100 feet across. Seen near older homes and in parks, the leaves of the monkeypod drop in February and March. Its wood is a favorite of woodworking artisans.

Night-Blooming Cereus Look along rock walls for this spectacular night-blooming flower. Originally from Central America, this vinelike member of the cactus family has green scalloped edges and produces foot-long white flowers that open as darkness falls and wither as the sun rises. The plant also bears an edible red fruit.

Orchids To many minds, nothing says Hawaii more than orchids. The most widely grown variety and the major source of flowers for leis and garnish for tropical libations is the vanda orchid. The vandas used in Hawaii's commercial flower industry are generally lavender or white, but they grow in a rainbow of colors, shapes, and sizes. The orchids used for corsages are the large, delicate cattleya; the ones used in floral arrangements you'll probably see them in your hotel lobby are usually dendrobiums.

Pandanus (*Hala*) Called *hala* by Hawaiians, pandanus is native to Polynesia. Thanks to its thick trunk, stiltlike supporting roots, and crown of long, swordlike leaves, the *hala* tree is easy to recognize. In what is quickly becoming a dying art, Hawaiians weave the *lau* (leaves) of the *hala* into hats, baskets, mats, bags, and the like.

Plumeria Also known as frangipani, this sweet-smelling, five-petal flower, found in clusters on trees, is the most popular choice of lei makers. The Singapore plumeria has five creamy-white petals, with a touch of yellow in the center. Another popular variety, ruba with flowers from soft pink to flaming red is also used in leis. When picking plumeria, be careful of the sap from the flower it's poisonous and can stain clothes.

Protea Originally from South Africa, this unusual oversize shrub comes in more than 40 different varieties. The flowers of one species resemble pincushions; those of another look like a bouquet of feathers. Once dried, proteas will last for years.

Silversword This very uncommon and unusual plant is seen only on the Big Island and in the Haleakala Crater on Maui. This rare relative of the sunflower family blooms between July and September. The silversword in bloom is a fountain of red-petaled, daisylike flowers that turn silver soon after blooming.

Taro Around pools, near streams, and in neatly planted fields, you'll see these green heart-shaped leaves, whose dense roots are a Polynesian staple. The ancient Hawaiians pounded the roots into poi. Originally from Sri Lanka, taro is not only a food crop, but is also grown for ornamental reasons.

The Fauna of the Islands

When the first Polynesians arrived in Hawaii between A.D. 500 and 800, scientists say they found some 67 varieties of endemic Hawaiian birds, a third of which are now believed to be extinct. They did not find any reptiles, amphibians, mosquitoes, lice, fleas, or even cockroaches.

There were only two endemic mammals: the hoary bat and the monk seal. The hoary bat must have accidentally blown to Hawaii at some point, from either North or South America. It can still be seen during its early evening forays, especially around the Kilauea Crater on the Big Island.

The Hawaiian monk seal, a relative of warm-water seals found in the Caribbean and the Mediterranean, was nearly slaughtered into extinction for its skin and oil during the 19th century. These seals have recently experienced a minor population explosion; sometimes they even turn up at various beaches throughout the state. They're protected under federal law by the Marine Mammal Protection Act. If you're fortunate enough to see a monk seal, just look; don't disturb one of Hawaii's living treasures.

The first Polynesians brought a few animals from home: dogs, pigs, and chickens (all were for eating), as well as rats (stowaways). All four species are still found in the Hawaiian wild today.

Birds

More species of native birds have become extinct in Hawaii in the last 200 years than anywhere else on the planet. Of 67 native species, 23 are extinct and 30 are endangered. Even the Hawaiian crow, the alala, is threatened.

The aeo, or Hawaiian stilt a 16-inch-long bird with a black head, black coat, white underside, and long pink legs can be found in protected wetlands such as the Kanaha Wildlife Sanctuary (where it shares its natural habitat with the Hawaiian coot) and Kealia Pond on Maui.

The nene is Hawaii's state bird. It's being brought back from the brink of extinction through strenuous protection laws and captive breeding. A relative of the Canada goose, the nene stands about 2 feet high and has a black head and yellow cheeks. The approximately 500 nene in existence can be seen in only three places: on Maui at Haleakala

National Park, on the Big Island at Mauna Kea State Recreation Area bird sanctuary, and on the slopes of Mauna Kea.

The Hawaiian short-eared owl, the pueo, which grows to between 12 and 17 inches, can be seen at dawn and dusk. According to legend, spotting a pueo is a good omen.

Leapin' Lizards!

Geckos are harmless, soft-skinned, insect-eating lizards that come equipped with suction pads on their feet, enabling them to climb walls and windows to reach tasty insects such as mosquitoes and cockroaches. You'll see them on windows outside a lighted room at night or hear their cheerful chirp.

Sea Life

Approximately 680 species of fish are known to inhabit the waters around the Hawaiian Islands. Of those, approximately 450 species stay close to the reef and inshore areas.

Coral The reefs surrounding Hawaii are made up of various coral and algae. The living coral grows through sunlight that feeds specialized algae, which, in turn, allow the development of the coral's calcareous skeleton. The reef, which takes thousands of years to develop, attracts and supports fish and crustaceans, which use it for food and habitat.

Mother Nature can batter the reef with a strong storm, but humans have proven far more destructive.

The corals most frequently seen in Hawaii are hard, rocklike formations named for their familiar shapes: antler, cauliflower, finger, plate, and razor coral. Some coral appears soft, such as tube coral; it can be found in the ceilings of caves. Black coral, which resembles winter-bare trees or shrubs, is found at depths of more than 100 feet.

Reef Fish Of the approximately 450 types of reef fish here, about 27% are native to Hawaii and are found nowhere else in the world. During the millions of years it took for the islands to sprout up from the sea, ocean currents mainly from Southeast Asia carried thousands of marine animals and plants to Hawaii's reef; of those, approximately 100 species adapted and thrived. You're likely to spot one or more of the following fish while underwater.

* Angelfish can be distinguished by the spine, located low on the gill plate. These fish are very shy; several species live in colonies close to coral.

* Blennies are small, elongated fish, ranging from 2 to 10 inches long, with the majority in the 3- to 4-inch range. Blennies are so small that they can live in tide pools; you might have a hard time spotting one.

* Butterflyfish, among the most colorful of the reef fish, are usually seen in pairs (scientists believe they mate for life) and appear to spend most of their day feeding. There are 22 species of butterflyfish, of which three (bluestripe; lemon, or milletseed; and multiband, or pebbled butterflyfish) are endemic. Most butterflyfish have a dark band through the eye and a spot near the tail resembling an eye, meant to confuse their predators (moray eels love to lunch on them).

* Moray and conger eels are the most common eels seen in Hawaii. Morays are usually docile except when provoked or when there's food around. Unfortunately, some morays have been fed by divers and now associate divers with food; thus, they can become aggressive. But most morays like to keep to themselves. While morays may look menacing, conger eels look downright happy, with big lips and pectoral fins (situated so that they look like big ears) that give them the appearance of a perpetually smiling face. Conger eels have crushing teeth so they can feed on crustaceans; because they're sloppy eaters, they usually live with shrimp and crabs that feed off the crumbs they leave.

* Parrotfish, one of the largest and most colorful of the reef fish, can grow up to 40 inches long. They're easy to spot their front teeth are fused together, protruding like buck teeth that allow them to feed by

scraping algae from rocks and coral. The rocks and coral pass through the parrotfish's system, resulting in fine sand. In fact, most of the white sand found in Hawaii is parrotfish waste; one large parrotfish can produce a ton of sand a year. Native parrotfish species include yellowbar, regal, and spectacled.

* Scorpion fish are what scientists call "ambush predators": They hide under camouflaged exteriors and ambush their prey. Several kinds sport a venomous dorsal spine. These fish don't have a gas bladder, so when they stop swimming, they sink that's why you usually find them "resting" on ledges and on the ocean bottom. They're not aggressive, but be very careful where you put your hands and feet in the water so as to avoid those venomous spines.

* Surgeonfish, sometimes called tang, get their name from the scalpel-like spines located on each side of the body near the base of the tail. Several surgeonfish, such as the brightly colored yellow tang, are boldly colored; others are adorned in more conservative shades of gray, brown, or black. The only endemic surgeonfish and the most abundant in Hawaiian waters is the convict tang, a pale white fish with vertical black stripes (like a convict's uniform).

* Wrasses are a very diverse family of fish, ranging in length from 2 to 15 inches. Wrasses can change gender from female to male. Some

have brilliant coloration that changes as they age. Several types of wrasse are endemic to Hawaii: Hawaiian cleaner, shortnose, belted, and gray (or old woman).

Game Fish Hawaii is known around the globe as the place for big-game fish marlin, swordfish, and tuna. Six kinds of billfish are found in the offshore waters around the islands: Pacific blue marlin, black marlin, sailfish, broadbill swordfish, striped marlin, and shortbill spearfish. Hawaii billfish range in size from the 20-pound shortbill spearfish and striped marlin to the 1,805-pound Pacific blue marlin, the largest marlin ever caught with rod and reel in the world.

Tuna ranges in size from small (1 lb. or less) mackerel tuna used as bait (Hawaiians call them *oioi*) to 250-pound yellowfin ahi tuna. Other local species of tuna are big-eye, albacore, kawakawa, and skipjack.

Other types of fish, also excellent for eating, include mahimahi (also known as dolphin fish or dorado), in the 20- to 70-pound range; rainbow runner, from 15 to 30 pounds; and wahoo (ono), from 15 to 80 pounds. Shoreline fishermen are always on the lookout for trevally (the state record for a giant trevally is 191 lb.), bonefish, ladyfish, threadfin, leatherfish, and goatfish. Bottom fishermen pursue a range of snapper red, pink, gray, and others as well as sea bass (the state record is a whopping 563 lb.) and amberjack (which weigh up to 100 lb.).

Whales Humpback whales are popular visitors that come to Hawaii to mate and calve every year, beginning in November and staying until spring April or so when they return to Alaska. On every island, you can take winter whale-watching cruises that will let you observe these magnificent leviathans up close. You can also spot them from shore humpbacks grow to up to 45 feet long, so when one breaches (jumps out of the water), you can see it for miles.

Humpbacks are among the biggest whales found in Hawaiian waters, but other whales such as pilot, sperm, false killer, melon-headed, pygmy killer, and beaked can be seen year-round, especially in the calm waters off the Big Island's Kona Coast.

Sharks Yes, there *are* sharks in Hawaii, but you more than likely won't see one unless you're specifically looking. About 40 different species of sharks inhabit the waters surrounding Hawaii, ranging from the totally harmless whale shark (at 60 ft., the world's largest fish), which has no teeth and is so docile that it frequently lets divers ride on its back, to the not-so-docile, extremely uncommon great white shark. The most common sharks seen in Hawaii are white-tip or gray reef sharks (about 5 ft. long) and black-tip reef sharks (about 6 ft. long).

Hawaii's Ecosystem Problems

Officials at Hawaii Volcanoes National Park on the Big Island saw a potential problem a few decades ago with people taking a few rocks home with them as "souvenirs." To prevent this problem from escalating, the park rangers created a legend that the fiery volcano goddess, Pele, would punish these souvenir seekers with bad luck. There used to be a display case in the park's visitor center filled with letters from people who had taken rocks from the volcano, relating stories of all the bad luck that followed. Most begged Pele's forgiveness and instructed the rangers to please return the rock to the exact location that was its original home.

Unfortunately, Hawaii's other ecosystem problems can't be handled as easily.

Marine Life Hawaii's beautiful and abundant marine life has attracted so many visitors that they threaten to overwhelm it. A great example of this is Molokini, a small crater off the coast of Maui. Twenty-five years ago, one or two small six-passenger boats made the trip once a day to Molokini; today it's not uncommon to sight 20 or more boats, each carrying 20 to 49 passengers, moored inside the tiny crater. One tour operator has claimed that, on some days, it's so crowded that you can actually see a slick of suntan oil floating on the surface of the water.

Hawaii's reefs have faced increasing impact over the years as well. Runoff of soil and chemicals from construction, agriculture, and erosion can blanket and choke a reef, which needs sunlight to survive. Human contact with the reef can also upset the ecosystem. Coral, the basis of the reef system, is very fragile; snorkelers and divers grabbing onto it can break off pieces that took decades to form. Feeding the fish can also upset the balance of the ecosystem (not to mention upsetting the digestive systems of the fish). In areas where they're fed, the normally shy reef fish become more aggressive, surrounding divers and demanding food.

Flora The rainforests are among Hawaii's most fragile environments. Any intrusion from hikers carrying seeds on their shoes to the rooting of wild boars can upset the delicate balance of these complete ecosystems. In recent years, development has moved closer and closer to the rainforests. On the Big Island, people have protested the invasion of bulldozers and the drilling of geothermal wells in the Wao Kele O Puna rainforest for years.

Fauna The biggest impact on the fauna in Hawaii is the decimation of native birds by feral animals, which have destroyed the birds' habitats, and by mongooses that have eaten the birds' eggs and young. Government officials are vigilant about snakes because of the potential damage they can do to the remaining bird life.

A recent pest introduced to Hawaii is the coqui frog. That loud noise you hear after dark, especially on the eastern side of the Big Island and various parts of Maui, including the Kapalua Resort area and on the windward side of the island, is the cry of the male coqui frog looking for a mate. A native of Puerto Rico, where the frogs are kept in check by snakes, the coqui frog came to Hawaii in some plant material, found no natural enemies, and has spread across the Big Island and Maui. A chorus of several hundred coqui frogs is deafening (it's been measured at 163 decibels, or the noise level of a jet engine from 100 ft.). In some places, like Akaka Falls, on the Big Island, there are so many frogs that they are now chirping during daylight hours.

Hawaii's Most Dangerous Invaders

There's trouble in Paradise serious trouble. Invasive species not native to Hawaii have destroyed native forests, killed the majority of the native birds, obliterated decades-old indigenous trees, and wiped out endemic fish found nowhere else on the planet.

The flora and fauna in Hawaii, the most isolated chain in the world, never developed defensive properties to warn off predators because there were no predators. Today, there are more endangered species per square mile in Hawaii than any other place on the planet.

- ➢ **Rats.** Rats came to Hawaii either on outrigger canoes steered by the Polynesians or on the whaling ships that showed up in the 1800's (or possibly both). Either way, the result was that rats ate birds' eggs and destroyed their habitat in the native forests.

- ➢ **Mongooses.** The small Indian mongoose was brought to Hawaii by sugar planters in 1883 as a solution to the rat problem. Unfortunately, no one considered that rats are nocturnal and the mongoose is not. Instead of killing rats, mongooses quickly started feasting on the eggs and chicks of native birds.

- ➢ **Pigs.** The Polynesians brought pigs with them to Hawaii. Feral pigs have since had an impact on nearly every native plant community in Hawaii. They root for food, eating native plants; invasive plants then establish themselves in the disturbed soil. The holes they leave behind fill with water, allowing mosquitoes carrying avian malaria to breed. With destruction of native vegetation comes the destruction of native bird and insect populations as well.

- ➢ **Erythrina gall wasp.** This tiny wasp came to Hawaii in recent years. It lays its eggs in the leaves and stems of wiliwili trees, creating an outbreak of tumors (galls) on the leaves. The infected tree dies, and the wind carries diseased leaves off to infect more wiliwili trees.

- **Gorilla seaweed.** In the 1970's, scientists introduced this edible seaweed to Hawaiian waters thinking it would make a good aquaculture crop. Since then this quickly growing seaweed has taken over several reefs, forming large, thick mats that overgrow and kill coral and other seaweeds, essentially smothering the reefs.

- **Tilapia.** Blame the scientists for this one too. This fish was introduced to Hawaii as an aquaculture crop. The problem this that tilapia can survive in both salt and fresh water, and feeds on almost anything from algae to insects. In particular tilapia have had damaging effects on Hawaii's native shrimp and gobies.

- **Man.** From clear cutting land (destroying Hawaii's native forests and all the plant, bird and insect species found there) to polluting the pristine waters with agricultural and other chemicals, to filling in sand at beaches, to creating harbors, to channeling streams, man's impact on the islands is unequaled.

Planning a Trip

Maui has so many places to explore, things to do, sights to see it can be bewildering to plan your trip with so much vying for your attention. Where to start? I strongly advise you to fly directly into Maui; doing so can save you a 2-hour layover in Honolulu and another plane ride.

For many, Maui inhabits the sweet spot. It's a tangle of lovely contradictions, with a Gucci heel on one foot and a *puka*-shell anklet on the other. Culturally, it's a mix of farmers, *paniolo* (Hawaiian cowboys), aspiring chefs, artists, New Age healers, and big wave riders. The landscape runs the gamut from sun-kissed golden beaches and fragrant rainforests to the frigid, wind-swept summit of Haleakala. Sure, more traffic lights sprout up around the island every year and spurts of development have turned cherished landmarks into mere memories. But even as Maui transforms, its allure remains.

Essentials

Arriving

By Plane--If you think of the island of Maui as the shape of a person's head and shoulders, you'll probably arrive near its neck, at Kahului Airport (OGG). Many airlines offer direct flights to Maui from the mainland U.S., including Hawaiian Airlines (www.hawaiianair.com; tel. 800/367-5320), Alaska Airlines (www.alaskaair.com; tel. 800/252/7522), United Airlines (www.united.com; tel. 800/241-6522),

American Airlines (www.aa.com; tel. 800/433-7300), Delta Air Lines (www.delta.com; tel. 800/221-1212), and U.S. Airways (www.usairways.com;tel. 800/428-4322). The only international flights to Maui originate in Canada, via Air Canada (www.aircanada.com; tel. 888/247-2262) and West Jet(www.westjet.com; tel. 888/937-8538), which both fly from Vancouver.

Other major carriers stop in Honolulu, where you'll catch an interisland flight to Maui on Hawaiian Airlines. (At present it's the only airline offering inter-island flights on jet aircraft.)

A small commuter service, Mokulele Airlines (www.mokuleleairlines.com; tel. 866/260-7070), recently expanded its routes to include flights from Honolulu to Kahului Airport and to Maui's two other airstrips. If you're staying in Lahaina or Kaanapali, you might consider flying in or out of Kapalua–West Maui Airport (JHM). From this tiny, one-pony airfield, it's only a 10- to 15-minute drive to most hotels in West Maui, as opposed to an hour or more from Kahului.Same story with Hana Airport (HNM): Flying directly here will save you a 3-hour drive.

Mokulelealso flies between Maui and Lanai, Molokai, and the Big Island. Check-in is a breeze: no security lines (unless leaving from Honolulu). You'll be weighed, ushered onto the tarmac, and welcomed aboard a nine-seat Cessna. The plane flies low, and the views between the islands are outstanding.

- ➢ Landing at Kahului--If you're renting a car, proceed to the car-rental desks just beyond baggage claim. All of the major rental companies have branches at Kahului. Each rental agency has a shuttle that will deliver you to the car lot a half-mile away.

If you're not renting a car, the cheapest way to exit the airport is the Maui Bus(www.mauicounty.gov/bus; tel. 808/871-4838). For $2 it will deposit you at any one of the island's major towns. Simply cross the street at baggage claim and wait under the awning. The next cheapest option is Roberts Hawaii Maui Airport Shuttle(www.airportmauishuttle.com; tel. 808/877-0907), which operates an on-demand airport shuttle. You can call upon arrival, but you'll get better rates and a written confirmation if you book online. Plan to pay $18 (one-way) to Kahului, $38 to Wailea, $53 to Kaanapali, and $73 to Kapalua—but know that prices drop significantly if you share the shuttle with other riders. SpeediShuttle (www.speedishuttle.com; tel. 877/242-5777) also services Kahului Airport, between 6am and 11pm daily. Rates are $39 (one-way) to Wailea, $54 to Kaanapali, and $74 to Kapalua. You'll need to book in advance.

Getting Around

By Car--The simplest way to see Maui is by rental car; public transit is still in its infancy here. All of the major car-rental firms—including Alamo, Avis, Budget, Dollar, Enterprise, Hertz, National, and Thrifty—have agencies on Maui. If you're on a budget or traveling with sports gear, you can rent an older vehicle by the week from Kimo's Rent-a-Car (www.kimosrentacar.com; tel. 808/280-6327, ext. 5

Maui has only a handful of major roads, and you can expect a traffic jam or two heading into Kihei, Lahaina, or Paia. In general, the roads hug the coastlines; one zigzags up to Haleakala's summit. When asking locals for directions, don't bother using highway numbers; residents know the routes by name only.

Traffic advisory: Be alert on the Honoapiilani Highway (Hwy. 30) en route to Lahaina. Drivers ogling whales in the channel between Maui and Lanai often slam on the brakes and cause major tie-ups and accidents. Because this is the only main road connecting the west side to the rest of the island, if there is an accident, flooding, a rock slide, or any other road hazard, traffic can back up for 1 to 8 hours (no joke). So before you set off, check with Maui County for road closure advisories (www.co.maui.hi.us; tel. 808/986-1200). The most up-to-date info can be found on its Twitter feed (@CountyofMaui) or that of a local news agency (@MauiNow).

- ➢ By Motorcycle--Feel the wind on your face and smell the salt air as you tour the island on a Harley, available for rent from Cycle City Maui, 150 Dairy Rd., Kahului (www.cyclecitymaui.com; tel. 808/831-2698). Rentals start at $99 a day.

- ➢ By Taxi--Because Maui's various destinations are so spread out, taxi service can be quite expensive and should be limited to travel within a neighborhood. Alii Taxi (tel. 808/661-3688) offers 24-hour service island-wide. Call Kihei Wailea Taxi (tel. 808/879-3000) if you need a ride in South Maui. Metered rate is $3 per mile.

- ➢ By Bus--The Maui Bus (www.mauicounty.gov/bus; tel. 808/871-4838) is a public/private partnership that provides convenient and affordable public transit to various communities across the island. Air-conditioned buses service 13 routes, including several that stop at the airport. All routes operate daily, including holidays. Fares are $2. Suitcases (one per passenger) and bikes are allowed; surfboards and sandboards are not.

Entry Requirements & Customs
Passports

Virtually every air traveler entering the U.S. is required to show a passport. All persons, including U.S. citizens, traveling by air between the United States and Canada, Mexico, Central and South America, the Caribbean, and Bermuda are required to present a valid passport. *Note:* U.S. and Canadian citizens entering the U. S. at land and sea ports of entry from within the Western Hemisphere must now also present a passport or other documents compliant with the Western Hemisphere Travel Initiative (WHTI; visit www.getyouhome.gov for details). Children 15 and under may continue entering with only a U.S. birth certificate, or other proof of U.S. citizenship.

Australia Australian Passport Information Service (tel. 131-232, or visit www.passports.gov.au).

Canada Passport Office, Department of Foreign Affairs and International Trade, Ottawa, ON K1A 0G3 (tel. 800/567-6868; www.ppt.gc.ca).

Ireland Passport Office, Setanta Centre, Molesworth Street, Dublin 2 (tel. 01/671-1633; www.foreignaffairs.gov.ie).

New Zealand Passports Office, Department of Internal Affairs, 47 Boulcott St., Wellington, 6011 (tel. 0800/225-050 in New Zealand or 04/474-8100; www.passports.govt.nz).

United Kingdom Visit your nearest passport office, major post office, or travel agency or contact the Identity and Passport Service (IPS), 89 Eccleston Square, London, SW1V 1PN (tel. 0300/222-0000; www.ips.gov.uk).

United States To find your regional passport office, check the U.S. State Department website (travel.state.gov/passport) or call the National Passport Information Center (tel. 877/487-2778) for automated information.

Visas

The U.S. State Department has a Visa Waiver Program (VWP) allowing citizens of the following countries to enter the United States without a visa for stays of up to 90 days: Andorra, Australia, Austria, Belgium, Brunei, Czech Republic, Denmark, Estonia, Finland, France, Germany, Greece, Hungary, Iceland, Ireland, Italy, Japan, Latvia, Liechtenstein, Lithuania, Luxembourg, Malta, Monaco, the Netherlands, New Zealand, Norway, Portugal, San Marino, Singapore, Slovakia, Slovenia, South Korea, Spain, Sweden, Switzerland, and the United Kingdom. (Note: This list was accurate at press time; for the most up-to-date list of countries in the VWP, consult http://travel.state.gov/visa.) Even though a visa isn't necessary, in an effort to help U.S. officials check travelers against terror watch lists before they arrive at U.S. borders, visitors from VWP countries must register online through the Electronic System for Travel Authorization (ESTA) before boarding a plane or a boat to the U.S.

Travelers must complete an electronic application providing basic personal and travel eligibility information. The Department of Homeland Security recommends filling out the form at least three days before traveling. Authorizations will be valid for up to two years or until the traveler's passport expires, whichever comes first. Currently, there is a $14 fee for the online application. Existing ESTA registrations remain valid through their expiration dates. Note: Any passport issued on or after October 26, 2006, by a VWP country must be an e-Passport for VWP travelers to be eligible to enter the U.S. without a visa. Citizens of these nations also need to present a round-trip air or cruise ticket upon arrival.

E-Passports contain computer chips capable of storing biometric information, such as the required digital photograph of the holder. If your passport doesn't have this feature, you can still travel without a visa if the valid passport was issued before October 26, 2005, and includes a machine-readable zone; or if the valid passport was issued between October 26, 2005, and October 25, 2006, and includes a digital photograph. For more information, go to http://travel.state.gov/visa. Canadian citizens may enter the United States without visas, but will need to show passports and proof of residence.

Citizens of all other countries must have (1) a valid passport that expires at least 6 months later than the scheduled end of their visit to the U.S.; and (2) a tourist visa.

For information about U.S. visas go to http://travel.state.gov/visa. Or go to one of the following websites:

Australian citizens can obtain up-to-date visa information from the U.S. Embassy Canberra, Moonah Place, Yarralumla, ACT 2600 (tel. 02/6214-5600) or by checking the U.S. Diplomatic Mission's website at http://canberra.usembassy.gov/visas.html.

British subjects can obtain up-to-date visa information by calling the U.S. Embassy Visa Information Line (tel. 09042-450-100 from within the U.K. at £1.20 per minute; or 866/382-3589 from within the U.S. at a flat rate of $16, payable by credit card only) or by visiting the "Visas to the U.S." section of the American Embassy London's website at http://london.usembassy.gov/visas.html.

Irish citizens can obtain up-to-date visa information through the U.S. Embassy Dublin, 42 Elgin Rd., Ballsbridge, Dublin 4 (tel. 1580-47-VISA

[8472] from within the Republic of Ireland at €2.40 per minute; http://dublin.usembassy.gov).

Citizens of New Zealand can obtain up-to-date visa information by contacting the U.S. Embassy New Zealand, 29 Fitzherbert Terrace, Thorndon, Wellington (tel. 644/462-6000; http://newzealand.usembassy.gov).

Customs

For details regarding U.S. Customs and Border Protection, consult your nearest U.S. embassy or consulate, or U.S. Customs (www.customs.gov).

You cannot take home fresh fruit, plants, or seeds (including some leis) unless they are sealed. You cannot seal and pack them yourself.

For information on what you're allowed to bring home, contact one of the following agencies:

U.S. Citizens: U.S. Customs and Border Protection, 1300 Pennsylvania Ave., NW, Washington, DC 20229 (tel. 877/287-8667; www.customs.gov).

Canadian Citizens: Canada Border Services Agency (tel. 800/461-9999 in Canada or 204/983-3500; www.cbsa-asfc.gc.ca).

U.K. Citizens: HM Revenue & Customs (tel. 0845/010-9000 or 020/8929-0152 from outside the U.K.; www.hmce.gov.uk).

Australian Citizens: Australian Customs and Border Protection Service (tel. 1300/363-263; www.customs.gov.au).

New Zealand Citizens: New Zealand Customs Service (tel. 04/473-6099 or 0800/428-786; www.customs.govt.nz).

Medical Requirements

Unless you're arriving from an area known to be suffering from an epidemic (particularly cholera or yellow fever), inoculations or vaccinations are not required for entry into the United States.

Getting Around

By Car

Hawaii has some of the lowest car-rental rates in the country. (An exception is the island of Lanai, where they're very expensive.) To rent a car in Hawaii, you must be at least 25 years of age and have a valid driver's license and credit card. Note: If you're visiting from abroad and plan to rent a car in the United States, keep in mind that foreign driver's licenses are usually recognized in the U.S., but you should get an international one if your home license is not in English.

At Maui's airport in Kahului you'll find most major car-rental agencies, including Alamo, Avis, Budget, Dollar, Enterprise, Hertz, National, and Thrifty. It's almost always cheaper to rent a car at the airport than in Waikiki or through your hotel (unless there's one already included in your package deal).

Rental cars are usually at a premium on Kauai, Molokai, and Lanai and may be sold out on the neighbor islands on holiday weekends, so be sure to book well ahead.

Gasoline Gas prices in Maui, always much higher than on the U.S. mainland, vary from island to island. At this writing, average prices for regular gas in Maui are about $3.99 per gallon (except in Hana where gas was $4.49).On Molokai gas was $4.57 and on Lanai gas was $4.99. Note: Taxes are already included in the printed price.

Insurance Hawaii is a no-fault state, which means that if you don't have collision-damage insurance, you are required to pay for all damages before you leave the state, whether or not the accident was your fault. Your personal car insurance may provide rental-car coverage; check before you leave home. Bring your insurance identification card if you decline the optional insurance, which usually costs from $12 to $20 a day. Obtain the name of your company's local claim representative before you go. Some credit card companies also provide collision-damage insurance for their customers; check with yours before you rent.

Driving Rules Hawaii state law mandates that all car passengers must wear a seat belt, and all infants must be strapped into a car seat. You'll pay a $50 fine if you don't buckle up. Pedestrians always have the right of way, even if they're not in the crosswalk. You can turn right on red after a full and complete stop, unless otherwise posted.

Road Maps The best and most detailed maps for activities are published by Franko Maps (www.frankosmaps.com); they feature a host of island maps, plus a terrific "Hawaiian Reef Creatures Guide" for snorkelers curious about those fish they spot under water. Free road maps are published by This Week Magazine, a visitor publication available on Maui.

Another good source is the University of Hawaii Press maps, which include a detailed network of island roads, large-scale insets of towns, historical and contemporary points of interest, parks, beaches, and hiking trails. If you can't find them in a bookstore near you, contact University of Hawaii Press, 2840 Kolowalu St., Honolulu, HI 96822 (tel. 808/956-8255; www.uhpress.hawaii.edu). For topographic and other maps of the islands, go to the Hawaii Geographic Society, 49 S. Hotel

St., Honolulu (tel. 800/538-3950 or 808/538-3952; hawaiigeographicsociaty@gmail.com).

Stay off the Cellphone Talking on a cellphone while driving in Maui is a big no-no. Fines range from $92 to $150. One woman on the island of Oahu was even ticketed for talking on a cellphone while she was parked on the side of the road! Save yourself the money, don't use the cell while you are driving

Fast Facts

Fast Facts Maui

Dentists--Emergency dental care is available at Hawaii Family Dental, 1847 S. Kihei Rd., Kihei (tel. 808/874-8401), or at Aloha Lahaina Dentists, 134 Luakini St. (in the Maui Medical Group Bldg.), Lahaina (tel. 808/661-4005).

Doctors--Urgent Care West Maui, Whalers Village, 2435 Kaanapali Pkwy., Suite H-7 (next to the Westin), Kaanapali (www.westmauidoctors.com; tel. 808/667-9721), is open 365 days a year; no appointment is necessary. In Kihei, call Urgent Care Maui,1325 S. Kihei Rd., Suite 103 (at Lipoa St., across from Star Market), Kihei (tel. 808/879-7781), which is open daily from 7am to 9pm.

Emergencies--Call tel. 911 for police, fire, and ambulance service. District stations are located in Lahaina (tel. 808/661-4441) and in Hana (tel. 808/248-8311).

Hospitals--In Central Maui, Maui Memorial Hospital is at 221 Mahalani, Wailuku (tel. 808/244-9056). East Maui's Hana Community Health Center is at 4590 Hana Hwy. (www.hanahealth.org; tel. 808/248-8294). In Upcountry Maui, Kula Hospital is at 204 Kula Hwy., Kula (tel. 808/878-1221).

Internet Access--Many places offer free Wi-Fi. Starbucks (www.starbucks.com/store-locator) provides Internet service in its stores in Kahului, Pukalani, Lahaina, and Kihei.

Post Office--To find the nearest post office, call tel. 800/ASK-USPS. In Lahaina, there are branches at the Lahaina Civic Center, 1760 Honoapiilani Hwy., and at the Lahaina Shopping Center, 132 Papalaua St. In Kahului, there's a branch at 138 S. Puunene Ave., and in Kihei, there's one at 1254 S. Kihei Rd.

Weather--For the current weather, the Haleakala National Park weather, or the marine and surf conditions, call the National Weather Service's Maui forecast (tel. 866/944-5025) or visit www.prh.noaa.gov/hnl and click on the island of Maui.

When to Go

Most visitors don't come to Maui when the weather's best on the island; rather, they come when it's at its worst everywhere else. Thus, the high season when prices are up and resorts are often booked to capacity is generally from mid-December through March or mid-April. The last 2 weeks of December, in particular, are the prime time for travel to Hawaii. If you're planning a holiday trip, make your reservations as early as possible, expect crowds, and prepare to pay top dollar for accommodations, car rentals, and airfare.

The off season, when the best rates are available and the islands are less crowded, is spring (mid-Apr to mid-June) and fall (Sept to mid-Dec) a paradox because these are the best seasons to be in Hawaii, in terms of reliably great weather. If you're looking to save money, or if you just want to avoid the crowds, this is the time to visit. Hotel rates and airfares tend to be significantly lower, and good packages are often available.

Note: If you plan to come to Maui between the last week in April and early May, be sure you book your accommodations, interisland air reservations, and car rentals in advance. In Japan, the last week of April is called Golden Week because three Japanese holidays take place one after the other.

Due to the large number of families traveling in summer (June-Aug), you won't get the fantastic bargains of spring and fall. However, you'll still do much better on packages, airfare, and accommodations than you will in the winter months.

Climate

Because Hawaii lies at the edge of the tropical zone, it technically has only two seasons, both of them warm. There's a dry season that corresponds to summer (Apr-Oct) and a rainy season in winter (Nov-Mar). It rains every day somewhere in the islands any time of the year, but the rainy season sometimes brings enough gray weather to spoil your tanning opportunities. Fortunately, it seldom rains in one spot for more than 3 days straight.

The year-round temperature doesn't vary much. At the beach, the average daytime high in summer is 85°F (29°C), while the average daytime high in winter is 78°F (26°C); nighttime lows are usually about 10° cooler. But how warm it is on any given day really depends on where you are on the island.

Each island has a leeward side (the side sheltered from the wind) and a windward side (the side that gets the wind's full force). The leeward sides (the west and south) are usually hot and dry, while the windward sides (east and north) are generally cooler and moist. When you want arid, sunbaked, desertlike weather, go leeward. When you want lush, wet, junglelike weather, go windward.

Maui is also full of microclimates, thanks to its interior valleys, coastal plains, and mountain peaks. It can be hot, dry, and sunny on the island's leeward side in Lahaina and Kihei, but it's downright chilly at 3,000 feet and above in the upcountry region of Kula there is snow on top of 10,000-foot Haleakala. On the windward side, an abundance of rain is what makes Kahului, Haiku, and Hana so verdant. If the weather doesn't suit you where you are, just head to the other side of the island or into the hills.[0]

On rare occasions, the weather can be disastrous, as when Hurricane Iniki crushed Kauai in September 1992 with 225-mph winds. Tsunamis have swept Hilo and the south shore of Oahu. But those are extreme exceptions. Mostly, one day follows another here in glorious, sunny procession, each quite like the other.

Holidays

When Hawaii observes holidays (especially those over a long weekend), travel between the islands increases, interisland airline seats are fully booked, rental cars are at a premium, and hotels and restaurants are busier.

Federal, state, and county government offices are closed on all federal holidays.

State and county offices are also closed on local holidays, including Prince Kuhio Day (Mar 26), honoring the birthday of Hawaii's first delegate to the U.S. Congress; King Kamehameha Day (June 11), a statewide holiday commemorating Kamehameha the Great, who united the islands and ruled from 1795 to 1819; and Admissions Day (third Fri in Aug), which honors the admittance of Hawaii as the 50th state on August 21, 1959.

Other special days celebrated in Hawaii by many people but that involve no closing of federal, state, and county offices are the Chinese New Year (which can fall in Jan or Feb), Girls' Day (Mar 3), Buddha's Birthday (Apr 8), Father Damien's Day (Apr 15), Boys' Day (May 5), Samoan Flag Day (in Aug), Aloha Festivals (Sept-Oct), and Pearl Harbor Day (Dec 7).

The Island in Brief
Central Maui
This flat, often windy corridor between Maui's two volcanoes is where you'll most likely arrive it's the site of the main airport. It's also home to the majority of the island's population, the heart of the business community, and the local government (courts, cops, and county/state

government agencies). You'll find good shopping and dining bargains here but very little in the way of accommodations.

Kahului This is "Dream City," home to thousands of former sugar-cane workers whose dream in life was to own their own homes away from the sugar plantations. There's wonderful shopping here (especially at discount stores), and a couple of small hotels near the airport are convenient for 1-night stays if you have a late arrival or early departure, but this is not a place to spend your entire vacation.

Wailuku Wailuku is like a time capsule, with its faded wooden storefronts, old plantation homes, shops straight out of the 1940s and 1950s, and relaxed way of life. While most people race through on their way to see the natural beauty of Iao Valley, this quaint little town is worth a brief visit, if only to see a real place where real people actually appear to be working at something other than a suntan. This is the county seat, so you'll see people in suits on important missions in the tropical heat. Beaches surrounding Wailuku are not great for swimming, but the town has a spectacular view of Haleakala Crater, great budget restaurants, some interesting bungalow architecture, a Frank Lloyd Wright building, a wonderful historic B&B, and the always-endearing Bailey House Museum.

West Maui

This is the fabled Maui you see on postcards. Jagged peaks, green velvet valleys, a wilderness full of native species the majestic West Maui Mountains are the epitome of earthly paradise. The beaches here are some of Hawaii's best. And it's no secret: This stretch of coastline along Maui's "forehead," from Kapalua to the historic port of Lahaina, is the island's most bustling resort area (with south Maui close behind). Expect a few mainland-style traffic jams.

If you want to book a resort or condo on this coast, first consider what community you'd like to base yourself in. Starting at the southern end of west Maui and moving northward, the coastal communities look like this:

Lahaina This old seaport is a tame version of its former self, a raucous whaling town where sailors swaggered ashore in search of women and grog. Today, the vintage village teems with restaurants, T-shirt shops, and a gallery on nearly every block; parts of it are downright tacky, but there's still a lot of real history to be found amid the tourist development. Lahaina makes a great base for visitors: A few old hotels (such as the restored 1901 Pioneer Inn on the harbor), quaint bed-and-breakfasts, and a handful of oceanfront condos offer a variety of choices. This is the place to stay if you want to be in the center of things restaurants, shops, and nightlife but parking can be a problem.

Kaanapali Farther north along the west Maui coast is Hawaii's first master-planned family resort. Pricey midrise hotels line nearly 3 miles of lovely gold-sand beach; they're linked by a landscaped parkway and a walking path along the sand. Golf greens wrap around the slope between beachfront and hillside properties. Whalers Village a seaside mall with 48 shops and restaurants, plus the best little whale museum in Hawaii and other restaurants are easy to reach on foot along the oceanfront walkway or by resort shuttle, which also serves the small West Maui Airport just to the north. Shuttles also go to Lahaina , 3 miles to the south, for shopping, dining, entertainment, and boat tours. Kaanapali is popular with convention groups and families especially those with teenagers, who like all the action.

Honokowai, Kahana & Napili During the building binge of the 1970s, condominiums sprouted along this gorgeous coastline like mushrooms after a rain. Today, these older ocean-side units offer excellent bargains for astute travelers. The great location along sandy beaches, within minutes of both the Kapalua and Kaanapali resort areas, and close enough to the goings-on in Lahaina makes this area a great place to stay for value-conscious travelers. It feels more peaceful and residential than either Kaanapali or Lahaina.

In Honokowai and Mahinahina, you'll find mostly older units that tend to be cheaper. There's not much shopping here (mostly convenience stores), but you'll have easy access to the shops and restaurants of Kaanapali.

Kahana is a little more upscale than Honokowai and Mahinahina. Most of its condos are big high-rise types, newer than those immediately to the south. You'll find a nice selection of shops and restaurants (including the Maui branch of Roy's) in the area, and Kapalua-West Maui Airport is nearby.

Napili is a much-sought-after area for condo seekers: It's quiet; has great beaches, restaurants, and shops; and is close to Kapalua. Units are generally more expensive here (although I've found a few hidden gems at affordable prices).

Kapalua North beyond Kaanapali and the shopping centers of Napili and Kahana, the road starts to climb and the vista opens up to fields of golden-green pineapple and manicured golf fairways. A country lane lined with Pacific pines that leads toward the sea brings you to Kapalua. It's the very exclusive domain of the luxurious Ritz-Carlton Kapalua and expensive condos and villas, set on one of Hawaii's best white-sand beaches, next to two bays that are marine-life preserves (with fabulous surfing in winter).

Even if you don't stay here, you're welcome to come and enjoy Kapalua. The fancy hotel here provides public parking and beach access. The resort has an art school where you can learn local crafts, as well as a golf school, three golf courses, historic features, swanky condos and homes (many available for vacation rental at astronomical prices), and wide-open spaces that include a rainforest preserve all open to the general public.

Kapalua is a great place to stay put. However, if you plan to "tour" Maui, know that it's a long drive from here to get to many of the island's highlights. You might want to consider a more central place to stay even Lahaina is a 15-minute drive away.

South Maui

This is the hottest, sunniest, driest, most popular coastline on Maui for sun lovers Arizona by the sea. Rain rarely falls here, and temperatures stick around 85°F (29°C) year-round. On this former scrubland from Maalaea to Makena, where cacti once grew wild and cows grazed, there are now four distinctive areas Maalaea, Kihei, Wailea, and Makena and a surprising amount of traffic.

Maalaea If west Maui is the island's head, Maalaea is just under the chin. This windy oceanfront village centers on a small boat harbor (with a general store, a couple of restaurants, and a huge new mall) and the Maui Ocean Center, an aquarium/ocean complex. This quaint region offers several condominium units to choose from, but visitors staying here should be aware that it's almost always very windy. All the wind from the Pacific is funneled between the West Maui Mountains and Haleakala and comes out in Maalaea.

Kihei Kihei is less a proper town than a nearly continuous series of condos and minimalls lining South Kihei Road. This is Maui's best vacation bargain: Budget travelers swarm like sun-seeking geckos over the eight sandy beaches along this scalloped, condo-packed 7-mile stretch of coast. Kihei is neither charming nor quaint; what it lacks in aesthetics, though, it more than makes up for in sunshine, affordability, and convenience. If you want a latte in the morning, fine beaches in the afternoon, and Hawaii Regional Cuisine in the evening all at reasonable prices head to Kihei.

Wailea Just 3 decades ago, this was wall-to-wall scrub kiawe trees, but now Wailea is a manicured oasis of multimillion-dollar resort hotels along 2 miles of palm-fringed gold coast. It's like Beverly Hills by the sea, except California never had it so good: Wailea has warm, clear water full of tropical fish; year-round golden sunshine and clear blue skies; and hedonistic pleasure palaces on 1,500 acres of black-lava shore indented by five beautiful beaches. It's amazing what a billion dollars can do.

This is the playground of the stretch-limo set. The planned resort development practically a well-heeled town has a shopping village, three prized golf courses of its own and three more in close range, and a tennis complex. A growing number of large homes sprawl over the upper hillside, some offering excellent bed-and-breakfast units at reasonable prices. The resorts along this fantasy coast are spectacular, to say the least. Next door to the Four Seasons, the most elegant, is the Grand Wailea Resort Hotel & Spa, a public display of ego by Tokyo mogul Takeshi Sekiguchi, who dropped $600 million in 1991 to create his own minicity. Stop in and take a look it's so gauche, you've gotta see it.

Appealing natural features include the coastal trail, a 3-mile round-trip path along the oceanfront with pleasing views everywhere you look out to sea and to the neighboring islands, or inland to the broad lawns and gardens of the hotels. The trail's south end borders an extensive garden of native coastal plants, as well as the ruins of ancient lava-rock houses juxtaposed with elegant oceanfront condos. But the chief attractions, of course, are those five outstanding beaches (the best is Wailea Beach).

Makena After passing through well-groomed Wailea, suddenly the road enters raw wilderness. After Wailea's overdone density and overmanicured development, the thorny landscape is a welcome relief. Although beautiful, this is an end-of-the-road kind of place: It's a long drive from Makena to anywhere on Maui. If you're looking for an activities-filled vacation or you want to tour a lot of the island, you might want to try somewhere else, or you'll spend most of your time in the car. But if you crave a quiet, relaxing respite, where the biggest trip of the day is from your bed to the gorgeous, pristine beach, Makena is the place.

Beyond Makena, you'll discover Haleakala's last lava flow, which ran to the sea in 1790; the bay named for French explorer La Pérouse; and a chunky lava trail known as the King's Highway, which leads around Maui's empty south shore past ruins and fish camps. Puu Olai stands like Oahu's Diamond Head on the shore, where a sunken crater shelters tropical fish and empty gold-sand beaches stand at the end of dirt roads.

Upcountry Maui

After a few days at the beach, you'll probably take notice of the 10,000-foot mountain in the middle of Maui. The slopes of Haleakala (House of the Sun) are home to cowboys, growers, and other country people who wave at you as you drive by. They're all up here enjoying the crisp air, emerald pastures, eucalyptus, and flower farms of this tropical Olympus there's even a misty California redwood grove. You can see a thousand tropical sunsets reflected in the windows of houses old and new, strung along a road that runs like a loose hound from Makawao, an old cowboy-turned-New Age village, to Kula, where the road leads up to the crater and Haleakala National Park. The rumpled, two-lane blacktop of Hwy. 37 narrows on the other side of Tedeschi Vineyards and Winery, where wine grapes and wild elk flourish on the Ulupalakua Ranch, the biggest on Maui. A stay upcountry is usually affordable, a chance to commune with nature, and a nice contrast to the sizzling beaches and busy resorts below.

Makawao Until recently, this small, two-street upcountry town consisted of little more than a post office, gas station, feed store, bakery, and restaurant/bar serving the cowboys and farmers living in the surrounding community; the hitching posts outside storefronts were really used to tie up horses. As the population of Maui started expanding in the 1970s, a health-food store sprang up, followed by boutiques, a chiropractic clinic, and a host of health-conscious restaurants. The result is an eclectic amalgam of old *paniolo* (cowboy) Hawaii and the baby-boomer trends of transplanted mainlanders. Hui No'eau Visual Arts Center, Hawaii's premier arts collective, is definitely worth a peek. The only accommodations here are reasonably priced bed-and-breakfasts, perfect for those who enjoy great views and don't mind slightly chilly nights.

Kula A feeling of pastoral remoteness prevails in this upcountry community of old flower farms, humble cottages, and newer suburban ranch houses with million-dollar views that take in the ocean, the isthmus, the West Maui Mountains, and, at night, the lights that run along the gold coast like a string of pearls from Maalaea to Puu Olai. Everything flourishes at a cool 3,000 feet (bring a jacket), just below the cloud line, along a winding road on the way up to Haleakala National Park. Everyone here grows something Maui onions, carnations, orchids, and proteas (those strange-looking blossoms that look like *Star Trek* props). The local B&Bs cater to guests seeking cool tropic nights, panoramic views, and a rural upland escape. Here you'll find the true peace and quiet that only rural farming country can offer yet you're still just 30 to 40 minutes away from the beach and an hour's drive from Lahaina.

East Maui

On the Road to Hana When old sugar towns die, they usually fade away in rust and red dirt. Not Paia. The tangled spaghetti of electrical, phone, and cable wires hanging overhead symbolizes the town's ability to adapt to the times it may look messy, but it works. Here, trendy restaurants, eclectic boutiques, and high-tech windsurf shops stand next door to a ma-and-pa grocery, a fish market, and storefronts that have been serving customers since plantation days. Hippies took over in the 1970s; although their macrobiotic restaurants and old-style artists' co-ops have made way for Hawaii Regional Cuisine and galleries featuring the works of renowned international artists, Paia still manages to maintain a pleasant granola vibe. The town's main attraction, though, is Hookipa Beach Park, where the wind that roars through the isthmus of Maui brings windsurfers from around the world. A few B&Bs are located just outside Paia in the tiny community of Kuau.

Ten minutes down the road from Paia and up the hill from the Hana Highway the connector road to the entire east side of Maui is Haiku. Once a pineapple-plantation village, complete with a cannery (now a shopping complex), Haiku offers vacation rentals and B&Bs in a quiet, pastoral setting: the perfect base for those who want to get off the beaten path and experience the quieter side of Maui, but don't want to feel too removed (the beach is only 10 min. away).

About 15 to 20 minutes past Haiku is the largely unknown community of Huelo. Every day, thousands of cars whiz by on the road to Hana;

most barely glance at the double row of mailboxes overseen by a fading Hawaii Visitors Bureau sign. But if you take the time to stop and head down the gun-metal road, you'll discover a hidden Hawaii a Hawaii of an earlier time, where Mother Nature is still sensual and wild, where ocean waves pummel soaring lava cliffs, and where an indescribable sense of serenity prevails. Huelo is not for everyone, but those who hunger for a place still largely untouched by "progress" should check in to a B&B or vacation rental here.

Hana Set between an emerald rainforest and the blue Pacific is a village probably best defined by what it lacks: golf courses, shopping malls, and McDonald's. Except for a gas station and a bank with an ATM, you'll find little of what passes for progress here. Instead, you'll discover the simple joys of fragrant tropical flowers, the sweet taste of backyard bananas and papayas, and the easy calm and unabashed small-town aloha spirit of old Hawaii. What saved "Heavenly" Hana from the inevitable march of progress? The 52-mile Hana Highway, which winds around 600 curves and crosses more than 50 one-lane bridges on its way from Kahului. You can go to Hana for the day from Kihei and Lahaina, it's a 3-hour drive (and a half century away) but 3 days are better. The tiny town has one hotel, a handful of great B&Bs, and some spectacular vacation rentals.

Calendar of Events

Please note that as with any schedule of upcoming events, the following information is subject to change; always confirm the details before you plan your trip around an event.

For an exhaustive list of events beyond those listed here, check http://events.frommers.com, where you'll find a searchable, up-to-the-minute roster of what's happening in cities all over the world.

January

PGA Championship, Kapalua Resort, Maui. Top PGA golfers compete for $1 million. Call tel. 808/669-2440 or go to www.kapaluamaui.com. First weekend in January.

EA Sports Maui Invitational Basketball Tournament, Lahaina Civic Center, Lahaina. Top college teams vie in this annual preseason tournament. Call tel. 847/850-1818 or go to www.mauiinvitational.com. Early January.

Chinese New Year, Maui. Lahaina town rolls out the red carpet for this important event with a traditional lion dance at the historic Wo Hing Temple on Front Street, accompanied by fireworks, food booths, and a host of activities. Call tel. 888/310-1117 or 808/667-9175 or go to www.visitlahaina.com. Also on Maui, at the Maui Mall in Kahului; call tel. 808/878-1888. Chinese New Year can fall in January or February;

2012 ushers in the year of the dragon on January 23; in 2013, the year of the snake comes in on February 10.

February

Kaanapali Champions Skins Game, Kaanapali Golf Courses, Maui. Longtime golfing greats participate in this four-man tournament for $770,000 in prize money. Call tel. 808/661-3271 or go to www.kaanapali-golf.com. Late January or early February.

Whale Day Celebration, Kalama Park, Kihei. A daylong celebration in the park, with a parade of whales, entertainment, a crafts fair, games, and food. Call tel. 808/249-8811 or go to www.visitmaui.com. Early or mid-February.

Ocean Arts Festival, Lahaina. The entire town of Lahaina celebrates the annual migration of Pacific humpback whales with this festival in Banyan Tree Park. Artists display their best ocean-themed art for sale, while Hawaiian musicians and hula troupes entertain. Enjoy marine-related activities, games, and a Creature Feature touch-pool exhibit for children. Call tel. 888/310-1117 or 808/667-9194 or go to www.visitlahaina.com. Mid-March.

March

Prince Kuhio Day Celebrations. Various festivals are held throughout Hawaii to celebrate the birth of Jonah Kuhio Kalanianaole, who was born on March 26, 1871, and elected to Congress in 1902. Molokai also hosts a 1-day celebration; call tel. 808/553-3876 or go to www.visitmolokai.com to learn more.

April

East Maui Taro Festival, Hana, Maui. Taro, a Hawaiian staple food, is celebrated through music, hula, arts, crafts, and, of course, food. Call tel. 808/264-1553 or go to www.tarofestival.org. Varying dates in April.

Buddha Day, Lahaina Jodo Mission, Lahaina, Maui. Each year on the first Saturday in April, this historic mission holds a flower festival pageant honoring the birth of Buddha. The first Saturday in April.

Celebration of the Arts, Ritz-Carlton Kapalua, Kapalua Resort, Maui. Contemporary and traditional artists give free hands-on lessons during this 4-day festival, which begins the Thursday before Easter. Call tel. 808/669-6200 or go to www.celebrationofthearts.org. Early April.

Polo Spring Season Begins. For a complete list of all the polo matches in the cool, upcountry area of Maui, call tel. 808/877-7744 or go to www.visitmaui.com.

David Malo Day, Lahainaluna High School, Lahaina. This daylong event, with hula and other Hawaiian cultural celebrations, commemorates

Hawaii's famous scholar and ends with a luau. Call tel. 808/662-4000 or go to www.visitmaui.com. Mid- or late April.

Banyan Tree Birthday Party, Lahaina. Come celebrate the birthday of Lahaina's famous Banyan Tree with a weekend of activities. Call tel. 888/310-1117 or 808/667-9175 or go to www.visitlahaina.com. Generally the end of April.

May

Outrigger Canoe Season, all islands. From May to September, canoe paddlers across the state participate in outrigger canoe races nearly every weekend. Call tel. 808/383-7798 or go to www.y2kanu.com for this year's schedule of events.

Lei Day Celebrations, various locations on all islands. May Day is Lei Day in Hawaii, celebrated with lei-making contests, pageantry, arts and crafts and music. For a list of Maui events go to www.visitmaui.com/maui/calendar, which includes the Lei Day Brothers Cazimero concert at the Castle Theatre (tel. 808/242-7469).

Maui Onion Festival, Whalers Village, Kaanapali, Maui. Everything you ever wanted to know about the sweetest onions in the world. There is food, entertainment, tasting, and the Maui Onion cook-off. Call tel. 808/661-4567 or go to www.whalersvillage.com/onionfestival.htm. Early May.

International Festival of Canoes, West Maui. At this celebration of the Pacific islands' seafaring heritage, events include canoe paddling and sailing regattas, a luau feast, cultural demonstrations, canoe-building exhibits, and music. Call tel. 888/310-1117. Mid- to late May.

June

Hawaiian Slack-Key Guitar Festival, Maui Arts & Cultural Center, Kahului, Maui. This festival features great music performed by the best musicians in Hawaii. It's 5 hours long and free. Call tel. 808/226-2697 or go to www.slackkeyfestival.com. Late June. Check the website for festivals on the other islands and their dates.

King Kamehameha Celebration, all islands. This state holiday (officially June 11, but celebrated on different dates on each island) features a massive floral parade, hoolaulea (party), and much more. Call tel. 808/667-9194 for Maui events, tel. 808/553-3876 for Molokai events, or go to http://hawaii.gov/dags/king_kamehameha_commission. Most events in 2012 will be held early to mid-June.

Kapalua Wine & Food Festival, Ritz-Carlton and various locations, Maui. One of Hawaii's best food-and-wine festivals features Hawaii's top chefs as well as international chefs and sommeliers showing off their culinary talents and wines from around the world. The event's

30th year will be 2012. Not to be missed. Call tel. 800/527-2582 or go to www.kapaluamaui.com. Early June.

Maui Film Festival, Wailea Resort, Maui. Five days and nights of screenings of premieres and special films, along with traditional Hawaiian storytelling, chants, hula, and contemporary music. It begins the Wednesday before Father's Day. Call tel. 808/579-9244 or go to www.mauifilmfestival.com. Mid-June.

July

Fourth of July. Lahaina holds an old-fashioned Independence Day celebration with fireworks lighting the night sky over Lahaina's roadstead. Call tel. 888/310-1117 or 808/667-9194 or go to www.visitlahaina.com. Kaanapali puts on a grand old celebration with live music, children's activities, and fireworks. Call tel. 808/661-3271.

Makawao Parade & Rodeo, Makawao, Maui. The annual parade and rodeo event has been taking place in this upcountry cowboy town for generations. Go to www.visitmaui.com. July 4.

Polo Season, Olinda Polo Field, Makawao. Polo matches featuring Hawaii's top players, often joined by famous international players, are held every Sunday at 1pm throughout the summer. Call tel. 808/877-7744 or go to www.mauipolo.com.

Bon Dance & Lantern Ceremony, Lahaina, Maui. This colorful Buddhist ceremony honors the souls of the dead. Call tel. 808/661-4304. Usually the first Saturday in July.

August

Hawaii State Windsurfing Championship, Kanaha Beach Park, Kahului, Maui. Top windsurfers compete. Call tel. 808/877-2111 or go to www.surfmaui.com. Late July or early August.

Tahiti Fete, War Memorial Gym, Wailuku, Maui. This is an annual festival with Tahitian dance competition, arts and crafts, and food. Call tel. 808/250-0737 or go to http://tahitifete.blogspot.com.

Admissions Day, all islands. This is a state holiday honoring the day (August 21, 1959) that Hawaii became the 50th state. All state-related facilities are closed. Third Friday in August.

September

Aloha Festivals, various locations on all islands. Parades and other events celebrate Hawaiian culture and friendliness throughout the state. Call tel. 808/878-1888 or go to www.festivalsofaloha.com.

A Taste of Lahaina, Lahaina Civic Center, Maui. Some 30,000 people show up to sample 40 signature entrees from Maui's premier chefs during this weekend festival, which includes cooking demonstrations, wine tastings, and live entertainment. The event begins Friday night with Maui Chefs Present, a dinner/cocktail party featuring about a dozen of Maui's best chefs. Call tel. 808/667-9175 or go to www.visitmaui.com. Second weekend in September.

Hana Relays, Hana Highway. Hundreds of runners, in relay teams, crowd the Hana Highway from Kahului to Hana (you might want to avoid the road on this day). Call tel. 808/243-9636 or go to www.virr.com. Early September.

Maui Marathon, Kahului to Kaanapali. Runners line up at the Maui Mall before daybreak and head off for Kaanapali. Call tel. 866/577-8379 or go to www.virr.com or www.mauimarathonhawaii.com. Mid- to late September.

Maui County Fair, War Memorial Complex, Wailuku, Maui. The oldest county fair in Hawaii features a parade, amusement rides, live entertainment, and exhibits. Call tel. 808/270-7626 or go to www.calendarmaui.com. Last weekend in September.

October

Aloha Festivals Hoolaulea, Lahaina. This all-day cultural festival, which marks the end of Maui's Aloha Festivals Week, is held at Banyan Tree Park and features Hawaiian food, music, and dance, along with arts and crafts on display and for sale. Call tel. 888/310-1117 or 808/667-9194 or go to www.visitlahaina.com. September or October.

November

Hawaii International Film Festival, various locations throughout the state. This cinema festival with a cross-cultural spin features filmmakers from Asia, the Pacific Islands, and the United States. Call tel. 808/792-1577 or go to www.hiff.org. Late October or early November.

December

Na Mele O Maui, Kaanapali, Maui. A traditional Hawaiian song competition for children in kindergarten through 12th grade, held in the ballroom of one of the Kaanapali Resort hotels. Admission is $5 donation. Call tel. 808/661-3271 or go to www.kaanapaliresort.com. First Friday in December.

Hui Noeau Christmas House, Makawao. The festivities in the beautifully decorated Hui mansion include shopping, workshops and art demonstrations, children's activities and visits with Santa, holiday music, fresh-baked goods, and local foods. Call tel. 808/572-6560 or go to www.huinoeau.com. Late November and early December.

Billabong Pro Maui, Honolua Bay at Kapalua Resort, Maui. The final Triple Crown women's surfing contest of the year, bringing together the best of the women's international surfing community. Call tel. 800/527-2582 or go to www.billabongpro.com. Early December.

Festival of Trees, Lahaina Cannery Mall, Lahaina. Look for decorated trees as well as entertainment. Call tel. 808/661-5304. Early December.

Lighting of the Banyan Tree, Lahaina. At 6:30pm, Lahaina's historic Banyan Tree is lit up with thousands of Christmas lights for the entire holiday season. Santa Claus makes an appearance, and choirs sing Christmas carols accompanied by hula. Kids can join a cookie workshop. Call tel. 808/667-9194 or 667-9194 or go to www.visitlahaina.com. Early December.

Tree Lighting Ceremony, Ritz-Carlton Kapalua, Kapalua Resort. With the flick of a switch, more than 250,000 sparkling lights illuminate a 25-foot holiday tree and dozens of pine and palm trees around the courtyards of the Ritz-Carlton Kapalua and throughout the resort. Call tel. 808/669-6200 or go to www.kapaluaresort.com. Early December.

Festival of Lights, all islands. On Maui, marching bands, floats, and Santa roll down Lahaina's Front Street in an annual parade. Molokai celebrates with a host of activities in Kaunakakai. Call tel. 808/667-9175 for Maui and go to www.visitmolokai.com for Molokai. Early December.

Old-Fashioned Holiday Celebration, Lahaina, Maui. This day of Christmas carolers, Santa Claus, live music and entertainment, a crafts fair, holiday baked goods, and activities for children takes place in the Banyan Tree Park on Front Street. Call tel. 888/667-9175 or go to www.visitlahaina.com. First weekend in December.

FirstLight; Academy Screening on Maui, Maui Arts & Cultural Center, Kahului, Maui. Major films are screened at this festival; past selections have included The Lord of the Rings: Return of *the* King, Mystic River, The Aviator, Hotel Rwanda, and many others. Not to be missed. Call tel. 808/579-9244 or 808/242-7469 or go to www.mauifilmfestival.com. Late December and early January.

Ongoing events on Maui

Every Friday night from 7 to 10pm, as part of Friday Night Is Art Night in Lahaina, the town's galleries open their doors for special shows, demonstrations, and refreshments. There are even strolling musicians wandering the streets.

If you're hungry for Hawaiian music, the Masters of Hawaiian Slack Key Guitar Series (tel. 888/669-3858; www.slackkey.com) features some of the great masters (and some Grammy Award winners) of this guitar style unique to the Hawaiian Islands. Concerts are held every

Wednesday night at 7:30pm at the Napili Kai Beach Resort. Tickets are $40; call in advance for reservations.

On the first and third weekends of the month, Hawaiian artists sell and share culture, arts, and crafts under the famous landmark Banyan Tree in Lahaina. On the other weekends, the Lahaina Arts Society holds an exhibit and sale of various works of art in the same place.

Every Wednesday at 5:30 and 7:30pm, the Maui Film Festival (tel. 808/572-3456or 579-9244; www.mauifilmfestival.com) presents outstanding contemporary and art films at the Maui Arts & Cultural Center, 1 Cameron Way (just off Kahului Beach Rd.), in Kahului.

You don't have to spend a good chunk of change and order two drinks to experience the Hawaiian art of hula. There are free hula performances every week. In Lahaina, they take place Saturday and Sunday at 1pm and Tuesday and Thursday at 7pm in the Lahaina Cannery Mall. In Kaanapali, they're held nightly, at 7 and 8pm at the Whalers Village; and every night at 6:30pm at the Kaanapali Beach Hotel. If you would like to try the hula yourself, there are free hula lessons at Whalers Village every Thursday from 3 to 4pm.

Maui's produce has long been a source of pride for islanders, check out Farmers' Markets around the island.

Tips on Accommodations

Maui offers all kinds of accommodations, from simple rooms in restored plantation homes and quaint cottages on the beach to luxurious oceanview condo units and opulent suites in beachfront resorts. Each type has its pluses and minuses, so before you book, make sure you know what you're getting into.

Hotels

In Maui, a "hotel" can indicate a wide range of options, from few or no on-site amenities to enough extras to qualify the place as a miniresort. Generally, a hotel offers daily maid service and has a restaurant, laundry facilities, a pool, and a sundries/convenience-type shop. Top hotels also have activities desks, concierge and valet services, room service, business centers, airport shuttles, bars and/or lounges, and perhaps a few more shops.

The advantages of staying in a hotel are privacy and convenience; the disadvantage is generally noise (either thin walls between rooms or loud music from a lobby lounge late into the night). Hotels are often a short walk from the beach rather than right on the beachfront (although there are exceptions).

Nickel-and-Dime Charges at High-Priced Hotels Several upscale resorts in Maui engage in a practice that I find distasteful and dishonest:

charging a so-called resort fee. This daily fee is added on to your bill for such "complimentary" items as a daily newspaper, local phone calls, and use of the fitness facilities amenities that the resort has been happily providing free to its guests for years. In most cases, you do not have an option to decline the resort fee in other words, this is a sneaky way to increase the nightly rate without telling you.

Resorts

In Hawaii, a resort offers everything a hotel does and more. You can expect direct beach access, with beach cabanas and lounge chairs; pools and a Jacuzzi; a spa and fitness center; restaurants, bars, and lounges; a 24-hour front desk; concierge, valet, and bellhop services; room service (often 24-hr.); an activities desk; tennis and golf; ocean activities; a business center; kids' programs; and more.

The advantages of a resort are that you have everything you could possibly want in the way of services and things to do; the disadvantage is that the price generally reflects this. And don't be misled by a name just because a place is called "ABC Resort" doesn't mean it actually *is* a resort. Make sure you're getting what you pay for.

Condos

The roominess and convenience of a condo which is usually a fully equipped, multiple-bedroom apartment makes this a great choice for families. Condominium properties in Maui generally consist of several apartments set in either a single high-rise or a cluster of low-rise units. Condos usually have amenities such as some maid service (ranging from daily to weekly; it may or may not be included in your rate), a pool, and an on-site front desk or a live-in property manager. Condos tend to be clustered in resort areas. There are some very high-end condos, but most are quite affordable, especially if you're traveling in a group.

The advantages of a condo are privacy, space, and conveniences which usually include a full kitchen, a washer and dryer, a private phone, and more. The downsides are the standard lack of an on-site restaurant and the density of the units (vs. the privacy of a single-unit vacation rental).

Bed & Breakfasts

Maui has a wide range of places that call themselves B&Bs: everything from a traditional B&B several bedrooms in a home, with breakfast served in the morning to what is essentially a vacation rental on an owner's property that comes with fixings for you to make your own breakfast. Make sure that the B&B you're booking matches your own mental picture. Note: Laundry facilities and private phones are not always available. If you have to share a bathroom, I've spelled it out in the listings; otherwise, you can assume that you will have your own.

The advantages of a traditional B&B are its individual style and congenial atmosphere, with a host who's often happy to act as your own private concierge. In addition, they're usually an affordable way to go. The disadvantages are lack of privacy, usually a set time for breakfast, few amenities, and generally no maid service. Also, B&B owners typically require a minimum stay of 2 or 3 nights, and it's often a drive to the beach.

B&B Etiquette In Maui, it is traditional and customary to remove your shoes before entering anyone's home. The same is true at most bed-and-breakfast facilities. If you consider this custom unpleasant, a B&B may not be for you. Maui also has a very strict no-smoking law (no smoking in public buildings, restaurants, bars, retail stores, and the like), and more and more hotels, resorts, condos, and vacation rentals generally do not allow smoking in the guest rooms (those hotels that still do allow smoking all have nonsmoking rooms available). The majority of bed-and-breakfasts forbid smoking. Be sure to check the policy of the establishment before you book.

Vacation Rentals

This is another great choice for families and for long-term stays. "Vacation rental" usually means that there will be no one on the property where you're staying. The actual accommodations can range from an apartment to an entire fully equipped house. Generally, vacation rentals allow you to settle in and make yourself at home for a while. They have kitchen facilities (at least a kitchenette), on-site laundry facilities, and a phone; some also come with such extras as a TV, VCR or DVD player, and stereo.

The advantages of a vacation rental are complete privacy, your own kitchen (which can save you money on meals), and lots of conveniences. The disadvantages are a lack of an on-site property manager and generally no maid service; often a minimum stay is required (sometimes as much as a week). If you book a vacation rental, be sure that you have a 24-hour contact to call if the toilet won't flush or you can't figure out how to turn on the air-conditioning.

Using a Booking Agency Versus Doing It Yourself

If you don't have the time to call several places yourself to make sure they offer the amenities you'd like, you might consider using a booking agency.

A statewide booking agent for B&Bs is Bed & Breakfast Hawaii (tel. 800/733-1632or 808/822-7771; fax 808/822-2723; www.bandbhawaii.com), offering a range of accommodations from vacation homes to bed-and-breakfasts, starting at $65 a night. For vacation rentals, contact Hawaii Beachfront Vacation Homes (tel. 808/247-3637; fax 808/235-2644; www.myhawaiibeachfront.com). Hawaii Condo Exchange(tel. 800/442-0404; www.hawaiicondoexchange.com) acts as a consolidator for condo and vacation-rental properties.

Getting There

By Plane
If you think of the island of Maui as the shape of a head and shoulders of a person, you'll probably arrive at its neck, at Kahului Airport (OGG). If you're headed for Molokai or Lanai, you'll have to connect through Honolulu.

As of press time, the following airlines fly directly from the U.S. mainland to Kahului: United Airlines offers daily nonstop flights from San Francisco and Los Angeles; Hawaiian Airlines has flights from San Diego, Portland, and Seattle; Alaska Airlines offers flights from Anchorage to Seattle to Kahului; American Airlines flies from Los Angeles and San Jose; Northwest Airlines flies from Oakland, California; Continental Airlines flies from Orange County, California; and Delta Air Linesoffers flights from San Francisco via Los Angeles.

Other carriers fly to Honolulu, where you'll have to pick up an interisland flight to Maui. (The airlines listed in the preceding paragraph also offer many more flights to Honolulu from additional cities on the mainland.) Hawaiian Airlines offers jet service from Honolulu.

Arriving at the Airport
If there's a long wait at baggage claim, step over to the state-operated Visitor Information Center, where you can ask about island activities and pick up brochures and the latest issue of This Week Maui, which features great regional maps of the islands. After collecting your bags from the poky, automated carousels, take a deep breath, proceed to the curbside rental-car pickup area, and wait for the appropriate rental-agency shuttle van to take you a half mile away to the rental-car checkout desk. (All major rental companies have branches at Kahului.)

If you're not renting a car, the cheapest way to get to your hotel is via SpeediShuttle(tel. 877/242-5777; www.speedishuttle.com), which can take you between Kahului Airport and all the major resorts between 6am and 11pm daily. You'll see taxis outside the airport terminal, but note that they are quite expensive expect to spend around $85 for a ride from Kahului to Kaanapali and $60 to Wailea.

If possible, avoid landing on Maui between 3 and 6pm, when the working stiffs on Maui are "pau work" (finished with work) and a major traffic jam occurs at the first intersection getting out of the airport.

Agricultural Screening at the Airports When you leave, baggage and passengers bound for the mainland must be screened by agricultural officials. Officials will confiscate local produce, like avocados, bananas, and mangoes, in the name of fruit-fly control. Pineapples, coconuts, and papayas inspected and certified for export; boxed flowers; leis without seeds; and processed foods (macadamia nuts, coffee, jams, dried fruit, and the like) will pass.

Interisland Flights

If you must go through Honolulu, you will need to get an interisland flight to Maui. Since the September 11, 2001, terrorist attacks the major interisland carriers have cut way back on the number of interisland flights. The airlines warn you to show up at least 90 minutes before your flight, and believe me, with all the security inspections, you will need all 90 minutes to catch your flight.

Hawaii has two major interisland carriers: Hawaiian Airlines (tel. 800/367-5320;www.hawaiianair.com) and go! (tel. 888/I-FLY-GO-2 [435-9462]; www.iflygo.com).

Visitors to Molokai and Lanai have three commuter airlines to choose from: Island Air(tel. 800/323-3345; www.islandair.com), tel. 888/I-FLY-GO-2 [435-9462] (www.iflygo.com), and PW Express (tel. 888/866-5022 or 808/873-0877; www.pacificwings.com) which all serve Hawaii's small interisland airports on Maui, Molokai, and Lanai. However, I have to warn you that I have not had stellar service on Island Air and recommend that you book another carrier.

Some large airlines offer transatlantic or transpacific passengers special discount tickets under the name Visit USA, which allows mostly one-way travel from one U.S. destination to another at very low prices. Unavailable in the U.S., these discount tickets must be purchased abroad in conjunction with your international fare. This system is the easiest, fastest, and cheapest way to see the country.

Cruising Through the Islands
If you're looking for a taste of several islands in a single week, consider Norwegian Cruise Line (tel. 800/327-7030; www.ncl.com), the only cruise line that operates year-round in Hawaii. Norwegian's 2,240-passenger ship Pride of America circles the Hawaiian Islands, stopping on the Big Island, Maui, Kauai, and Oahu; some itineraries even go to Fanning Island in the Republic of Kiribati before returning to Honolulu. The disadvantage of a cruise is that you won't be able to see any of the

islands in-depth or at leisure; the advantage is that you can spend your days exploring the island where the ship is docked and your nights aboard ship sailing to the next port of call.

Escorted & Package Tours

If all you want is a fabulous beach and a perfectly mixed mai tai, then Maui has what you're looking for. But the island's wealth of natural wonders is equally hard to resist; the year-round tropical climate and spectacular scenery tend to inspire almost everyone to get outside and explore.

If you don't have your own snorkel gear or other watersports equipment, or if you just don't feel like packing it, don't fret: Everything you'll need is available for rent.

Outdoor Etiquette Act locally, think globally, and carry out what you carry in. Find a trash container for all your litter (including cigarette butts; it's very bad form to throw them out of your car window or to use the beach as an ashtray). Observe KAPU (taboo) and NO TRESPASSING signs. Don't climb on ancient Hawaiian heiau (temple) walls or carry home rocks, all of which belong to the Hawaiian volcano goddess, Pele. Some say it's just a silly superstition, but each year the national and state park services get boxes of lava rocks in the mail that have been sent back to Hawaii by visitors who've experienced unusually bad luck.

Setting Out on Your Own Versus Using an Outfitter

There are two ways to go: Plan all the details before you leave and either rent gear or schlep your stuff 2,500 miles across the Pacific, or go with an outfitter or a guide and let someone else worry about the details.

Experienced outdoors enthusiasts may head to coastal campgrounds or even trek to the 10,000-foot-high summit of Haleakale on their own. But in Maui, it's often preferable to go with a local guide who is familiar with the conditions at both sea level and summit peaks, knows the land and its flora and fauna in detail, and has all the gear you'll need. It's also good to go with a guide if time is an issue or if you have specialized interests. If you really want to see native birds, for instance, an experienced guide will take you directly to the best areas for sightings. And many forests and valleys in the interior of the islands are either on private property or in wilderness preserves accessible only on guided tours. The downside? If you go with a guide, plan on spending at least $100 a day per person.

But if you have the time, already own the gear, and love doing the research and planning, try exploring on your own. This book discusses the best spots to set out on your own, from the top offshore snorkel and dive spots to great daylong hikes, as well as the federal, state, and county agencies that can help you with hikes on public property; I also list references for spotting birds, plants, and sea life. I recommend that you always use the resources available to inquire about weather, trail, or surf conditions; water availability; and other conditions before you take off on your adventure.

For hikers, a great alternative to hiring a private guide is taking a guided hike offered by the Nature Conservancy of Hawaii, PO Box 96, Honolulu, HI 96759 (tel. 808/572-7849 on Maui, or 808/553-5236 on Molokai); or the Hawaii Chapter of the Sierra Club, PO Box 2577, Honolulu, HI 96813 (tel. 808/579-9802 on Oahu; www.hi.sierraclub.org). Both organizations offer guided hikes in preserves and special areas during the year, as well as day- to weeklong work trips to restore habitats and trails and to root out invasive plants. It might not sound like a dream vacation to everyone, but it's a chance to see the "real" Hawaii including wilderness areas that are ordinarily off-limits.

All Nature Conservancy hikes and work trips are free (donations are appreciated). However, you must reserve a spot for yourself, and a deposit is required for guided hikes to ensure that you'll show up; your deposit is refunded when you do. The hikes are generally offered once a month on Maui, Molokai, and Lanai. For all islands, call the Oahu office for reservations. Write for a schedule of guided hikes and other programs.

The Sierra Club offers weekly hikes on Maui. They are led by certified Sierra Club volunteers and are classified as easy, moderate, or strenuous. These half- or all-day affairs cost $1 for Sierra Club members and $3 for nonmembers (bring exact change). For a copy of the club newsletter, which lists all outings and trail-repair work, send $2 to the address above.

For more information, contact the Hawaii Ecotourism Association (tel. 877/300-7058; www.hawaiiecotourism.org).

Using Activities Desks to Book Your Island Fun

If you're unsure of which activity or which outfitter or guide is the right one for you and your family, you might want to consider booking through a discount activities center or activities desk. Not only will they save you money, but good activities centers should also be able to help you find, say, the snorkel cruise that's right for you, or the luau that's most suitable for both you *and* the kids.

Remember, however, that it's in the activities agent's best interest to sign you up with outfitters from which they earn the most commission. Some agents have no qualms about booking you into any activity if it means an extra buck for them. If an agent tries to push a particular outfitter or activity too hard, be skeptical. Conversely, they'll try to steer you away from outfitters who don't offer big commissions. For example, Trilogy, the company that offers Maui's most popular snorkel cruises to Lanai (and the only one with rights to land at Lanai's Hulopoe Beach), offers only minimum commissions to agents and does not allow agents to offer any discounts at all. As a result, most activities desks will automatically try to steer you away from Trilogy.

Another word of warning: Stay away from activities centers that offer discounts as fronts for timeshare sales presentations. Using a free or discounted snorkel cruise or luau tickets as bait, they'll suck you into a 90-minute presentation and try to get you to buy into a Hawaii timeshare in the process. Because their business is timeshares, not activities, they won't be as interested in, or as knowledgeable about, which activities might be right for you. These shady deals seem to be particularly rampant on Maui.

There are a number of very reliable local activities centers on each of the neighbor islands. On Maui, your best bet is Tom Barefoot's

Cashback Tours, 250 Alamaha St., Kahului (tel. 800/895-2040 or 808/661-8889; www.tombarefoot.com). Tom offers a 10% discount on all tours, activities, and adventures if you pay using cash, a personal check, or traveler's checks. If you use a credit card, you'll get a 7% discount. Finally, you can reserve activities yourself and save the commission by booking via the Internet. Most outfitters offer 10% to 25% off their prices if you book online.

Getting Married

The silky warm weather, the starry nights, the gentle trade winds caressing your skin Maui is so romantic. That's probably why thousands of people get married on the island. Plus, after the ceremony, you're already on your honeymoon. And the members of your wedding party will most likely be delighted, since you've given them the perfect excuse for their own island vacation.

More than 20,000 marriages are performed annually on the islands; nearly half are for couples from somewhere else. The booming wedding business has spawned more than 70 companies that can help you organize a long-distance event and stage an unforgettable wedding, Hawaiian style or your style. However, you can also plan your own island wedding, even from afar, and not spend a fortune doing it.

The Paperwork

The state of Hawaii has some very minimal procedures for obtaining a marriage license. The first thing you should do is contact the Marriage License Office, State Department of Health Bldg., 54 S. High St., Wailuku, HI 96793 (tel. 808/984-8210;www.state.hi.us/doh/records/vr_marri.html), which is open Monday through Friday from 8am to 4pm. The office will no longer mail you the brochure Getting Married; you can download it from the website or contact a marriage-licensing agent closest to where you'll be staying in Hawaii (also listed on the website).

Once on Maui, the prospective bride and groom must go together to the marriage-licensing agent to get the license, which costs $60 and is good for 30 days. Both parties must be 15 years of age or older (anyone 15-17 years old must have proof of age, written consent of both parents, and written approval of the judge of the family court) and not more closely related than first cousins. That's it.

Gay couples cannot marry in Hawaii. After a protracted legal battle and much discussion in the state legislature, the Hawaii Supreme Court ruled that the state will not issue marriage licenses to same-sex couples.

Doing It Yourself

The marriage-licensing agents, who range from employees of the governor's satellite office in Kona to private individuals, are usually friendly, helpful people who can steer you to a nondenominational minister or marriage performer who's licensed by the state of Hawaii. These marriage performers are great sources of information for budget weddings. They usually know wonderful places to have a ceremony for free or for a nominal fee. For the names and addresses of marriage-licensing agents on Maui and Lanai, call tel. 808/984-8210; on Molokai, call tel. 808/553-3663.

If you don't want to use a wedding planner, but you do want to make arrangements before you arrive on Maui, my best advice is to get a copy of the daily newspaper, the Maui News, PO Box 550, Wailuku, HI 96793 (tel. 808/244-7691;www.mauinews.com). People willing and qualified to conduct weddings advertise in the classifieds. They're great sources of information, as they know the best places to have the ceremony and can recommend caterers, florists, and everything else you'll need.

Using a Wedding Planner
Wedding planners many of whom are marriage-licensing agents as well can arrange everything for you, from a small, private outdoor affair to a full-blown formal ceremony in a tropical setting. They

charge anywhere from $150 to a small fortune it all depends on what you want.

Planners on Maui include First Class Weddings (tel. 800/262-8433 or 808/877-1411; www.firstclassweddings.com), A Dream Wedding: Maui Style (tel. 800/743-2777 or 808/661-1777; fax 808/667-2042; www.adreamwedding.net), Romantic Maui Weddings (tel. 800/808-4144 or 808/874-6444; fax 808/879-5525; www.justmauied.com), and Dolphin Dream Weddings (tel. 800/793-2-WED[793-2933] or 808/661-8535; www.dolphindreamweddings.com). For a more complete list, contact the Maui Visitors and Convention Bureau (tel. 800/525-MAUI [6284]; www.visitmaui.com). Many of the big resorts have their own coordinators on staff as well.

Sustainable Travel & Ecotourism

If there is one place on the planet that seems ideally suited for ecotourism and sustainable travel, it's Hawaii, a place people visit because of the ecology the ocean, the beach, the mountains, and the overall beauty of the place. It seems only natural that the maintenance of its environment would be a concern, both to the people who live there and the visitors who come to enjoy all its ecosystem has to offer.

In fact, Hawaii has a long history of environmental stewardship. The ancient Hawaiians not only knew about sustainability, but also practiced it in their daily lives. They had to! When the ancient Hawaiians occupied the islands they did not have the luxury of "importing" goods from anywhere else. They had the land under their feet and the ocean to gain subsistence from, and those resources had to last not only for their own lifetime, but also for the lifetimes of generations to come. So these ancient people lived in harmony with the land and sea, and had a complex social structure that managed resources and forbid the taking of various resources during certain times of the year, to allow those resources to replenish themselves.

Now fast forward to the 21st century. Today we, the current stewards of the islands of Hawaii, are just beginning to appreciate just how wise and advanced the ancient Hawaiians were. In some ways, the state of Hawaii is a pioneer when it comes to the various ways it protects and saves its natural resources. (For example, Hawaii is second only to California in the number of marine reserves in the National System of Marine Protected Areas.) And yet in other ways, modern Hawaii still falls short of the ancient Hawaiians, whose unique system sustained, without imports, the entire population.

Ongoing Environmental Initiatives

The state of Hawaii has several excellent stewardship programs to preserve the ocean environment and its resources, such as Marine Life Conservation Districts (an ocean version of parks the waters surrounding Molokini is an example), Fishery Management Areas (where what you can take from the ocean is restricted), Fishery Replenishment Areas, and Estuarine Reserves. On land, there are corresponding programs to protect the environment, from the Soil and Water Conservation District to Watershed Reserves.

In the visitor industry, the majority of hotels have adopted green practices, not only to save the environment, but also to save them money. Nearly every hotel in the state will have a card in your room asking you to really consider if you need a new towel or if you can hang it up and use it one more day. Various statewide organizations have numerous programs recognizing hotels that are helping the environment, such as the Green Business Awards Program, which recently awarded Ritz-Carlton Kapalua for its use of core-less toilet paper rolls in bathrooms, the elimination of plastic ware in dining areas, the installation of sustainable bamboo floors in select facilities, and for offering sustainable dining featuring organic heirloom herbs and vegetables as well as local exotic fruit. The hotel also runs a Jacques Cousteau Ambassadors of the Environment program, which teaches guests about natural tide pools, the rainforest, humpback whales, and local ecosystems through interactive activities with trained naturalists. Another Maui hotel, the Fairmont Kea Lani, also was recognized in 2010 for its green practices, specifically for its "Recycling Cents Program," which donates money from recyclables to local charities raising some $20,000 in 2010; an improved laundry water recycling system, which has saved over 50 million gallons of water since installation in 2005; the use of automatic eco-MODE thermostats reducing air conditioning costs by 20%, biodegradable food containers, and rock salt treating systems in pools; and for serving sustainable cuisine in its restaurants.

Every island has recycling centers (varying from collection of recyclable bottles only to places that take everything); for a list of recycling centers close to where you will be staying, visit the website of the Hawaii State Department of Health(http://hi5deposit.com/redcenters.html).

Restaurants across Maui, including Market Fresh Bistro in Makawao; Merriman's in Kapalua; I'O, Pacific'O, Mala Ocean Tavern, and David Paul's in Lahaina; and Beverly Gannon's, Joe's, and Mala Wailea in Wailea, are using more local products and produce than ever. Many proudly tell you that all of their products were grown, grazed, or caught within 100 miles of their restaurant. You can support this effort by ordering local (drink Kona coffee, not a coffee from Central America; eat local fish, not imported seafood). Ask the restaurant which items on its menu are grown or raised on the island, then order the local items.

Below are some helpful hints travelers to Hawaii might want to keep in mind during their adventure to the islands, so that their ecological footprint on Hawaii will be minimal.

What Visitors Can Do in & Around the Ocean
1. Do not touch anything in the ocean. In fact, unless you are standing on the sandy bottom where the waves roll into shore, try not to walk or stand on the ocean floor. The no-touch rule of thumb is not only for your protection there are plenty of stinging, stabbing things out there that could turn your vacation into a nightmare but also for the protection of the marine environment. Coral is composed of living things, which take years to grow, and a careless brush of your hand or foot could destroy them. Fragile habitats for marine critters can be damaged forever by your heavy foot.

2. Do not feed the fish, or any other marine creature. They have their own food and diet, and they can be irreparably harmed by your good intentions if you feed them "people food" or, even worse, some "fish food" you have purchased.

3. Leave the ocean and beach area cleaner than you found it. If you see trash in the ocean (plastic bags, bottles, and so on) remove it. You may save the life of a fish, turtle, marine mammal, or even a seabird by removing that trash, which kills hundreds of marine inhabitants every year. The same thing is true of the beach: Pick up trash, even if it's not yours.

4. The beach is not an ashtray. Do not use the sand for your cigarette butts. How would you like someone using your living room carpet as his ashtray?

5. Look at, but don't approach, turtles or Hawaiian monk seals resting on the shoreline. The good news is that the number of turtles and Hawaiian monk seals is increasing. Visitors may not know it, but both are protected by law. You must stay 100 feet away from them. So take photos, but do not attempt to get close to the resting sea creatures (and no, they are not dead or injured, just resting).

6. If you plan to go fishing, practice catch and release. Let the fish live another day. Ask your charter boat captain if they practice catch and release; if they say no, book with someone else.

7. If you are environmentally conscious, I do not recommend that you rent jet skis because they have a significant environmental impact.

What Visitors Can Do on Land
1. Don't litter (this includes throwing a cigarette butt out of your car).

2. Before you go hiking, scrub your hiking shoes (especially the soles) to get rid of seeds and soil.

3. When hiking, carry a garbage bag so you can carry out everything you carried in, including your litter (and if you see other garbage on the trail, carry it out, too).

4. Stay on the trail. Wandering off a trail is not only dangerous to you (you can get lost, fall off overgrown cliffs, or get injured by stepping into a hidden hole), but you could possibly carry invasive species into the native forests.

5. Do not pick flowers or plants along your hike. Just leave the environment the way you found it.

Transportation Concerns
Rental Cars Most visitors coming to Hawaii seem to think "convertible" when they think of renting a car, or they think "SUV" for off-road adventures. If you're thinking "hybrid," you'll have to check your budget, because hybrids from car-rental agencies are not only hard to find, but also extremely expensive in Hawaii. Car-rental agencies do have a variety of cars to rent, though, and you can make a point of

selecting a car which get the best gas mileage. Also, ask for a white car, as they use less energy to air-condition that a dark-colored car.

Interisland Transportation Now that the interisland ferry, Superferry, has declared bankruptcy, the only option for interisland travel between most islands is via air. There are two exceptions, however. If you're traveling between Maui and Lanai, you may want to consider taking the passenger-only Expeditions Maui-Lanai Passenger Ferry (Commonly referred to as the Lanai Ferry.) If you're traveling between Maui and Molokai, you can take the passenger-only *Molokai Princess*. Not only are these ferries cheaper than air travel, but their impact on the environment is also less, especially when you consider that most airlines will route you from Maui to Honolulu, then from Honolulu on to either Molokai or Lanai.

General Resources for Green travel

The following websites provide valuable wide-ranging information on sustainable travel. For a list of even more sustainable resources, as well as tips and explanations on how to travel greener, visit Frommers.com/planning.

- ➢ Responsible Travel (www.responsibletravel.com) is a great source of sustainable travel ideas; the site is run by a spokesperson for ethical tourism in the travel industry.

Sustainable Travel International(www.sustainabletravelinternational.org) promotes ethical tourism practices and manages an extensive directory of sustainable properties and tour operators around the world.

- Carbonfund (www.carbonfund.org), TerraPass (www.terrapass.org) and Carbon Neutral (www.carbonneutral.org) provide info on "carbon offsetting," or offsetting the greenhouse gas emitted during flights.

- Greenhotels (www.greenhotels.com) recommends green-rated member hotels around the world that fulfill the company's stringent environmental requirements. Environmentally Friendly Hotels (www.environmentallyfriendlyhotels.com) offers more green accommodation ratings.

- Sustain Lane (www.sustainlane.com) identifies sustainable eating and drinking choices around the U.S.; also visit www.eatwellguide.org for tips on eating sustainably in the U.S. and Canada.

- Tread Lightly (www.treadlightly.org) provides information on animal-friendly issues throughout the world, and the Whale and

Dolphin Conservation Society(www.wdcs.org) offers information about the ethics of swimming with dolphins.

Money

Frommer's lists exact prices in the local currency. However, rates fluctuate, so before departing consult a currency exchange website such as www.oanda.com/convert/classic to check up-to-the-minute rates.

ATMs (Cashpoints) are everywhere in Maui at banks, supermarkets, Longs Drugs, and in some resorts and shopping centers. The Cirrus (tel. 800/424-7787;www.mastercard.com) and PLUS (tel. 800/843-7587; www.visa.com) networks span the country; you can find them even in remote regions. Go to your bank card's website to find ATM locations at your destination. Be sure you know your daily withdrawal limit before you depart.

Note: Many banks impose a fee every time you use a card at another bank's ATM, and that fee is often higher for international transactions (up to $5 or more) than for domestic ones (where they're rarely more than $2). In addition, the bank from which you withdraw cash may charge its own fee. To compare banks' ATM fees within the U.S., use www.bankrate.com. Visitors from outside the U.S. should also find out whether their bank assesses a fee on charges incurred abroad.

➢ Credit cards are accepted everywhere except taxicabs and some small restaurants and bed-and-breakfasts.

Money

Frommer's lists exact prices in the local currency. However, rates fluctuate, so before departing consult a currency exchange website such as www.oanda.com/convert/classic to check up-to-the-minute rates.

ATMs (Cashpoints) are everywhere in Maui at banks, supermarkets, Longs Drugs, and in some resorts and shopping centers. The Cirrus (tel. 800/424-7787;www.mastercard.com) and PLUS (tel. 800/843-7587; www.visa.com) networks span the country; you can find them even in remote regions. Go to your bank card's website to find ATM locations at your destination. Be sure you know your daily withdrawal limit before you depart.

Note: Many banks impose a fee every time you use a card at another bank's ATM, and that fee is often higher for international transactions (up to $5 or more) than for domestic ones (where they're rarely more than $2). In addition, the bank from which you withdraw cash may charge its own fee. To compare banks' ATM fees within the U.S., use www.bankrate.com. Visitors from outside the U.S. should also find out whether their bank assesses a fee on charges incurred abroad.

Credit cards are accepted everywhere except taxicabs and some small restaurants and bed-and-breakfasts.

Health & Safety

Hiking Safety

Hikers should always let someone know where they're heading, when they're going, and when they plan to return; too many hikers get lost in Hawaii because they don't let others know their basic plans. And make sure you know how strenuous the route and trail you will follow are don't overestimate your ability.

Before you head out, always check weather conditions with the toll-free National Weather Service (tel. 866/944-5025) on Maui. Do not hike if rain or a storm is predicted; flash floods are common in Hawaii. Hike with a pal, never alone. Plan to finish your hike at least an hour before sunset; because Hawaii is so close to the equator, it does not have a twilight period, and thus it gets dark quickly after the sun sets. Wear hiking boots, a sun hat, clothes to protect you from the sun and from getting scratches, and high-SPF sunscreen on all exposed areas of skin. Take plenty of water, a basic first aid kit, a snack, and a bag to pack out what you pack in. Stay on the trail. Watch your step. It's easy to slip off precipitous trails and into steep canyons. Many experienced hikers and boaters today pack a cellphone in case of emergency; just dial tel. 911.

Vog The volcanic haze dubbed vog is caused by gases released when molten lava from the continuous eruption of Kilauea volcano on the Big Island pours into the ocean. When the winds shift, vog travels over to Maui. Some people claim that long-term exposure to the hazy, smoglike air causes bronchial ailments, but it's highly unlikely to cause you any harm in the course of your visit.

Don't Get Burned: Smart Tanning Tips Hawaii's Caucasian population has the highest incidence of malignant melanoma (deadly skin cancer) in the world. And nobody is completely safe from the sun's harmful rays: All skin types and races can burn. To ensure that your vacation won't be ruined by a painful sunburn, be sure to wear a strong sunscreen that protects against both UVA and UVB rays at all times (look for zinc oxide, benzophenone, oxybenzone, sulisobenzone, titanium dioxide, or avobenzone in the list of ingredients). Wear a wide-brimmed hat and sunglasses. Keep infants under 6 months out of the sun completely, and slather older babies and children with strong sunscreen frequently.

If you do get a burn, aloe vera, cool compresses, cold baths, and benzocaine can help with the pain. Stay out of the sun until the burn is completely gone.

Ocean Safety

Because most people coming to Hawaii are unfamiliar with the ocean environment, they're often unaware of the natural hazards it holds. With just a few precautions, your ocean experience can be a safe and happy one. An excellent book is *All Stings Considered: First Aid and Medical Treatment of Hawaii's Marine Injuries,* by Craig Thomas and Susan Scott (University of Hawaii Press, 1997).

Note: Sharks are not a big problem in Hawaii; in fact, they appear so infrequently that locals look forward to seeing them. Since records have been kept, starting in 1779, there have been only about 100 shark attacks in Hawaii, of which 40% were fatal. Most attacks occurred after someone fell into the ocean from the shore or from a boat; in these cases, the sharks probably attacked after the person was dead. Here are the general rules for avoiding sharks: Don't swim at sunrise, at sunset, or where the water is murky due to stream runoff sharks may mistake you for one of their usual meals. And don't swim where there are bloody fish in the water, as sharks become aggressive around blood.

The waters in Hawaii can range from as calm as glass to downright frightening (during storms); conditions usually fall somewhere in between. In general, expect rougher conditions in winter than in summer. Some 90% of the world's population tends toward seasickness. If you've never been out on a boat, or if you've been seasick in the past, you might want to heed the following suggestions:

- The day before you go out on a boat avoid alcohol; caffeine; citrus and other acidic juices; and greasy, spicy, or hard-to-digest foods.
- Get a good night's sleep the night before.
- Take or use whatever seasickness prevention works best for you medication, an acupressure wristband, ginger-root tea or capsules, or any combination. But do it *before* you board; once you set sail, it's generally too late.
- While you're on the boat, stay as low and as near the center of the boat as possible. Avoid the fumes (especially if it's a diesel boat); stay out in the fresh air and watch the horizon. Do not read.
- If you start to feel queasy, drink clear fluids, like water, and eat something bland, such as a soda cracker.

The most common stings in Hawaii come from jellyfish, particularly Portuguese man-of-war and box jellyfish. Since the poisons they inject are very different, you need to treat each type of sting differently.

A bluish-purple floating bubble with a long tail, the Portuguese man-of-war is responsible for some 6,500 stings a year on Oahu alone. These stings, although painful and a nuisance, are rarely harmful; fewer than 1 in 1,000 requires medical treatment. The best prevention is to watch for these floating bubbles as you snorkel (look for the hanging tentacles below the surface). Get out of the water if anyone near you spots these jellyfish.

Reactions to stings range from mild burning and reddening to severe welts and blisters. All Stings Considered recommends the following treatment: First, pick off any visible tentacles with a gloved hand, a stick, or anything handy; then rinse the sting with salt- or freshwater and apply ice to prevent swelling and to help control pain. Avoid folk remedies like vinegar, baking soda, or urinating on the wound, which may actually cause further damage. Most Portuguese man-of-war stings will disappear by themselves within 15 to 20 minutes if you do nothing at all to treat them. Still, be sure to see a doctor if pain persists or a rash or other symptoms develop.

Transparent, square-shaped box jellyfish are nearly impossible to see in the water. Fortunately, they seem to follow a monthly cycle: Eight to 10 days after the full moon, they appear in the waters on the leeward side of each island and hang around for about 3 days. Also, they seem to sting more in the morning hours, when they're on or near the surface.

The stings can cause anything from no visible marks to hivelike welts, blisters, and pain lasting from 10 minutes to 8 hours. *All Stings Considered* recommends the following treatment: First, pour regular household vinegar on the sting; this will stop additional burning. Do not rub the area. For pain, apply an ice pack. Seek additional medical treatment if you experience shortness of breath, weakness, palpitations, muscle cramps, or any other severe symptoms. Most box-jellyfish stings disappear by themselves without any treatment.

A new product, just on the market is Jellyfish Squish, made by Coastal Solutions (tel. 912/353-3368; www.swimoutlet.com/Jellyfish-Squish). It has been getting rave reviews from ocean enthusiasts. It takes away the sting quickly. Best to order it online before you get to Hawaii. Most sea-related punctures come from stepping on or brushing against the needlelike spines of sea urchins (known locally as wana). Be careful when you're in the water; don't put your foot down (even if you have booties or fins on) if you can't clearly see the bottom. Waves can push you into wana in a surge zone in shallow water. The spines can even puncture a wet suit.

A sea urchin puncture can result in burning, aching, swelling, and discoloration (black or purple) around the area where the spines entered your skin. The best thing to do is to pull any protruding spines out. The body will absorb the spines within 24 hours to 3 weeks, or the remainder of the spines will work themselves out. Again, contrary to popular wisdom, do not urinate or pour vinegar on the embedded spines this will not help.

All cuts obtained in the marine environment must be taken seriously because the high level of bacteria present in the water can quickly cause the cut to become infected. The best way to prevent cuts is to wear a wet suit, gloves, and reef shoes. Never touch coral; not only can you get cut, but you also can damage a living organism that took decades to grow.

The symptoms of a coral cut can range from a slight scratch to severe welts and blisters. All Stings Considered recommends gently pulling the edges of the skin open and removing any embedded coral or grains of sand with tweezers. Next, scrub the cut well with freshwater. If pressing a clean cloth against the wound doesn't stop the bleeding, or the edges of the injury are jagged or gaping, seek medical treatment.

Everything You've Always Wanted to Know About Sharks The Hawaii State Department of Land and Natural Resources offers a website, www.hawaiisharks.com, that covers the biology, history, and culture of these carnivores. It also provides safety information and data on shark bites in Hawaii.

Enjoying the Ocean & Avoiding Mishaps The Pacific Whale Foundation has a free brochure called Enjoying Maui's Unique Ocean Environment that introduces visitors to Hawaii's ocean, beaches, tide pools, and reefs. Although written for Maui (with maps showing Maui's beaches), it's a great general resource on how to stay safe around the ocean, with hints on how to assess the weather before you jump into the water and the best ways to view marine wildlife. To get the brochure, call tel. 808/244-8390 or visit www.pacificwhale.org.

General Safety

Although tourist areas are generally safe, visitors should always stay alert, even in laid-back Maui (and especially in resort and beach areas). It's wise to ask the island tourist office if you're in doubt about which neighborhoods are safe. Avoid deserted areas, especially at night. Don't go into any city park at night unless there's an event that attracts a crowd. Generally speaking, you can feel safe in areas where there are many people and open establishments.

Avoid carrying valuables with you on the street, and don't display expensive cameras or electronic equipment. Hold on to your pocketbook, and place your billfold in an inside pocket. In theaters, restaurants, and other public places, keep your possessions in sight.

Remember also that hotels are open to the public and that at a large property, security may not be able to screen everyone entering. Always lock your room door don't assume that once inside your hotel, you're automatically safe.

Recently, burglaries of tourists' rental cars in hotel parking structures and at beach parking lots have become more common. Park in well-lighted and well-traveled areas, if possible. Never leave any packages or valuables visible in the car. If someone attempts to rob you or steal your car, do not try to resist the thief or carjacker report the incident to the police department immediately. Ask your rental agency about personal safety, and get written directions or a map with the route to your destination clearly marked.

Generally, Hawaii has the same laws as the mainland United States. Nudity is illegal in Hawaii. There are *no* legal nude beaches (I don't care what you have read). If you are nude on a beach (or anywhere) in Hawaii, you can be arrested.

Smoking marijuana also is illegal. Yes, there are lots of stories claiming that marijuana is grown in Hawaii, but the drug is illegal; if you attempt to buy it or light up, you can be arrested.

Tips for Families

Maui is paradise for children: beaches to run on, water to splash in, and unusual sights to see. Look for Frommer's Hawaii with Kids (Wiley Publishing, Inc.).

The larger hotels and resorts offer supervised programs for children and can refer you to qualified babysitters. By state law, hotels can only accept children ages 5 to 12 in supervised activities programs, but they often accommodate younger kids by simply hiring babysitters to watch over them. You can also contact People Attentive to Children (PATCH), which can refer you to babysitters who have taken a training course on child care. On Maui, call tel. 808/242-9232; on Molokai and Lanai, call tel. 800/498-4145; or visit www.patchhawaii.org.

Baby's Away (tel. 800/942-9030 or 808/344-2219; www.babysaway.com) rents cribs, strollers, highchairs, playpens, and infant seats. The staff will deliver whatever you need to wherever you're staying and pick it up when you're done.

Tips for Gay and Lesbian Travelers

Hawaii is known for its acceptance of all groups. The number of gay- or lesbian-specific accommodations on the islands is limited, but most properties welcome gays and lesbians like any other travelers.

On Maui check out the website for Out in Hawaii (www.outinhawaii.com), which offers "Queer Resources and Information for The State of Hawaii," with vacation ideas, a calendar of events, information on Hawaii, and even a chat room.

Tips for Senior Travelers

Always carry identification with proof of your age it can really pay off. Discounts for seniors are available at almost all of Maui's major attractions and occasionally at hotels and restaurants. The Outrigger hotel chain, for instance, offers travelers ages 50 and older a 20% discount off regular published rates and an additional 5% off for members of AARP. Always ask when making hotel reservations or buying tickets.

The U.S. National Park Service offers an America the Beautiful National Park and Federal Recreational Lands Pass Senior Pass (formerly the Golden Age Passport), which gives seniors 62 years or older lifetime entrance to all properties administered by the National Park Service (NPS) national parks, monuments, historic sites, recreation areas, and national wildlife refuges for a one-time processing fee of $10. The pass must be purchased in person at any NPS facility that charges an entrance fee. Besides free entry, the America the Beautiful Senior Pass offers a 50% discount on some federal-use fees charged for such facilities as camping, swimming, parking, boat launching, and tours. For more information, go to www.nps.gov/fees_passes.htm or call the United States Geological Survey (USGS), which issues the passes, at tel. 888/275-8747.

Tips for Travelers with Disabilities

Travelers with disabilities are made to feel very welcome in Maui. Hotels are usually equipped with wheelchair-accessible rooms, and tour companies provide many special services. The Hawaii Center for Independent Living, 414 Kauwili St., Ste. 102, Honolulu, HI 96817 (tel. 808/522-5400; fax 808/586-8129), can provide information.

The only travel agency in Hawaii specializing in needs for travelers with disabilities is Access Aloha Travel (tel. 800/480-1143;

www.accessalohatravel.com), which can book anything, including rental vans (available on Maui and Oahu only), accommodations, tours, cruises, airfare, and anything else you can think of.

Walking Tours

Historic Lahaina

Getting There: From Kahului Airport, take the Kuihelani Highway (Hwy. 38) to the intersection of Honoapiilani Highway (Hwy. 30), where you turn left. Follow Honoapiilani Highway to Lahaina and turn left on Lahainaluna Road. When Lahainaluna Road ends, make a left on Front Street. Dickenson Street is a block down.

Start: Front and Dickenson streets.

Finish: Same location.

Time: About an hour.

Best Time: Monday- Friday, 10am-3pm

Back when "there was no God west of the Horn," Lahaina was the capital of Hawaii and the Pacific's wildest port. Today it's a milder version of its old self mostly a hustle bustle of whale art, timeshares, and "Just Got Lei'd" T-shirts. I'm not sure the rowdy whalers would be pleased. But if you look hard, you'll still find the historic port town they loved, filled with the kind of history that inspired James Michener to write his best-selling epic novel *Hawaii*.

Members of the Lahaina Restoration Foundation have worked for 3 decades to preserve Lahaina's past. They have labeled a number of historic sites with brown-and-white markers; below, I provide explanations of the significance of each site as you walk through Lahaina's past.

Begin your tour at the:

1. Master's Reading Room

This coral-and-stone building looks just as it did in 1834, when Rev. William Richards and Rev. E. Spaulding convinced the whaling-ship captains that they needed a place for the ships' masters and captains, many of whom traveled with their families, to stay while they were ashore. The bottom floor was used as a storage area for the mission; the top floor, from which you could see the ships at anchor in the harbor, was for the visiting ships' officers.

Next door is the:

2. Baldwin Home Museum

Harvard-educated physician Rev. Dwight Baldwin, with his wife of just a few weeks, sailed to Hawaii from New England in 1830. Baldwin was first assigned to a church in Waimea, on the Big Island, and then to Lahaina's Wainee Church in 1838. He and his family lived in this house until 1871. The Baldwin Home and the Master's Reading Room are the oldest standing buildings in Lahaina, made from thick walls of coral and hand-milled timber. Baldwin also ran his medical office and his missionary activities out of this house.

On the other side of the Baldwin Home Museum is the former site of the:

3. Richards House

The open field is empty today, but it is the site of the former home of Lahaina's first Protestant missionary, Rev. William Richards. Richards went on to become the chaplain, teacher, and translator to Kamehameha III. He was also instrumental in drafting Hawaii's constitution and acted as the king's envoy to the United States and England, seeking recognition of Hawaii as an independent nation. After his death in 1847, he was buried in the Wainee Churchyard.

From here, cross Front Street and walk toward the ocean, with the Lahaina Public Library on your right and the green Pioneer Inn on your left, until you see the:

4. Taro Patch

The lawn in front of the Lahaina Public Library was once a taro patch stretching back to the Baldwin home. The taro plant was a staple of the Hawaiian diet: The root was used to make poi, and the leaves were used in cooking. At one time Lahaina looked like a Venice of the tropics, with streams, ponds, and waterways flooding the taro fields. As the population of the town grew, the water was siphoned off for drinking.

Walk away from the Lahaina Harbor toward the edge of the lawn, where you'll see the:

5. Hauola Stone

Hawaiians believed that certain stones placed in sacred places had the power to heal. *Kahuna* (priests) of medicine used stones like this to help cure illnesses.

Turn around and walk back toward the Pioneer Inn; look for the concrete depression in the ground, which is all that's left of the:

6. Brick Palace

This structure was begun in 1798 as the first Western-style building in Hawaii. King Kamehameha I had this 20*40-foot, two-story brick structure built for his wife, Queen Kaahumanu (who is said to have preferred a grass-thatched house nearby). Inside, the walls were constructed of wood and the windows were glazed glass. Kamehameha I lived here from 1801 to 1802, when he was building his war canoe, *Peleleu,* and preparing to invade Kauai. A handmade stone sea wall surrounded the palace to protect it from the surf. The building stood for 70 years. In addition to being a royal compound, it was also used as a meetinghouse, storeroom, and warehouse.

7. Pioneer Inn

Lahaina's first hotel was the scene of some wild parties at the start of the 20th century. George Freeland, of the Royal Canadian Mounted Police, tracked a criminal to Lahaina and then fell in love with the town. He built the hotel in 1901 but soon discovered that Lahaina didn't get a lot of visitors. To make ends meet, Freeland built a movie theater, which was wildly successful. The Pioneer Inn remained the only hotel in all of west Maui until the 1950s. You can stay at this restored building today.

From the Pioneer Inn, cross Hotel Street and walk along Wharf Street, which borders the harbor. On your left is the:

8. Banyan Tree

This ancient tree has witnessed decades of luau, dances, concerts, private chats, public rallies, and resting sojourners under its mighty boughs. It's hard to believe that this huge tree was only 8 feet tall when it was planted here.

Continue along Wharf Street. Near the edge of the park is the:

9. Courthouse

In 1858, a violent windstorm destroyed about 20 buildings in Lahaina, including Hale Piula, which served as the courthouse and palace of King Kamehameha III. It was rebuilt immediately, using the stones from the previous building. It served not only as courthouse, but also as custom house, post office, tax collector's office, and government offices. Upstairs on the second floor is the Lahaina Heritage Museum, with exhibits on the history and culture of Lahaina (free admission; open daily 9am-5pm).

Continue down Wharf Street to Canal Street. On the corner are the remains of the:

10. Fort

This structure once covered an acre and had 20-foot-high walls. In 1830, some whalers fired a few cannonballs into Lahaina in protest of Rev. William Richards's meddling in their affairs. (Richards had convinced Gov. Hoapili to create a law forbidding the women of Lahaina from swimming out to greet the whaling ships.) In response to this threat, the fort was constructed from 1831 to 1832 with coral blocks taken from the ocean where the Lahaina Harbor sits today. As a further show of strength, cannons were placed along the waterfront, where they remain today. Historical accounts seem to scoff at the "fort," saying it appeared to be more for show than for force. It was later used as a prison, until it was finally torn down in the 1850s; its stones were used for construction of the new prison, Hale Paahao.

Cross Canal Street to the:

11. Canal

Unlike Honolulu with its natural deepwater harbor, Lahaina was merely a roadstead with no easy access to the shore. Whalers would anchor in deep water offshore, then board smaller boats (which they used to chase down and harpoon whales) to make the passage over the reef to shore. If the surf was up, coming ashore could be dangerous. In the 1840s, the U.S. consular representative recommended digging a canal from one of the freshwater streams that ran through Lahaina and charging a fee to the whalers who wanted to obtain fresh water. In 1913, the canal was filled in to construct Canal Street.

Up Canal Street is the:

12. Government Market

A few years after the canal was built, the government built a thatched marketplace with stalls for Hawaiians to sell goods to the sailors. Merchants quickly took advantage of this marketplace and erected drinking establishments, grog shops, and other pastimes of interest nearby. Within a few years, this entire area became known as "Rotten Row."

Make a right onto Front Street and continue down the street, past Kamehameha III Elementary School. Across from the park is:

13. Holy Innocents Episcopal Church

When the Episcopal missionaries first came to Lahaina in 1862, they built a church across the street from the current structure. In 1909, the church moved to its present site, which was once a thatched house built for the daughter of King Kamehameha I. The present structure, built in 1927, features unique paintings of a Hawaiian Madonna and birds and plants endemic to Hawaii, executed by DeLos Blackmar in 1940.

Continue down Front Street, and at the next open field, look for the white stones by the ocean, marking the former site of the "iron-roofed house" called:

14. Hale Piula

In the 1830s, a two-story stone building with a large surrounding courtyard was built for King Kamehameha III. However, the king preferred sleeping in a small thatched hut nearby, so the structure was never really completed. In the 1840s, Kamehameha moved his capital to Honolulu and wasn't using Hale Piula, so it became the local courthouse. The windstorm of 1858, which destroyed the courthouse on Wharf Street, also destroyed the iron-roofed house. The stones from Hale Piula were used to rebuild the courthouse on Wharf Street.

Continue down Front Street; across from the 505 Front Street complex is:

15. Maluuluolele Park

This sacred spot to Hawaiians is now the site of a park and ball field. This used to be a village, Mokuhinia, with a sacred pond that was the home of a *moo* (a spirit in the form of a lizard), which the royal family honored as their personal guardian spirit. In the middle of the pond was a small island, Mokuula, home to Maui's top chiefs. After conquering Maui, Kamehameha I claimed this sacred spot as his own; he and his two sons, Kamehameha II and III, lived here when they were in Lahaina. In 1918, in the spirit of progress, the pond was drained and the ground leveled for a park.

Make a left onto Shaw Street and then another left onto Wainee Street. On the left side, just past the cemetery, is:

16. Wainee Church

This was the first stone church built in Hawaii (1828-32). At one time the church could seat some 3,000 people, albeit tightly packed together, complete with "calabash spittoons" for the tobacco-chewing Hawaiian chiefs and the ship captains. That structure didn't last long the 1858 windstorm that destroyed several buildings in Lahaina also blew the roof off the original church, knocked over the belfry, and picked up the church's bell and deposited it 100 feet away. The structure was rebuilt, but that too was destroyed this time by Hawaiians protesting the 1894 overthrow of the monarchy. Again the church was rebuilt, and again it was destroyed by fire in 1947. The next incarnation of the church was destroyed by yet another windstorm in 1951. The current church has been standing since 1953. Be sure to walk around to the back of the church: The row of palm trees on the ocean side includes some of the oldest palm trees in Lahaina.

Wander next door to the first Christian cemetery in Hawaii:

17. Waihee Cemetery

Established in 1823, this cemetery tells a fascinating story of old Hawaii, with graves of Hawaiian chiefs, commoners, sailors, and missionaries and their families (infant mortality was high then). Enter this ground with respect, because Hawaiians consider it sacred many members of the royal family are buried here, including Queen Keopuolani, who was wife of King Kamehameha I, mother of kings Kamehameha II and III, and the first Hawaiian baptized as a Protestant. Among the other graves are those of Rev. William Richards (the first missionary in Lahaina) and Princess Nahienaena (sister of kings Kamehameha II and III).

Continue down Waihee Street to the corner of Luakini Street and the:

18. Hongwanji Mission

The temple was originally built in 1910 by members of Lahaina's Buddhist sect. The current building was constructed in 1927, housing a temple and language school. The public is welcome to attend the New Year's Eve celebration, Buddha's birthday in April, and O Bon Memorial Services in August.

Continue down Wainee Street. Just before the intersection with Prison Street, look for the historical marker for:

19. David Malo's Home

Although no longer standing, the house that once stood here was the home of Hawaii's first scholar, philosopher, and well-known author. Educated at Lahainaluna School, his book on ancient Hawaiian culture, *Hawaiian Antiquities,* is considered *the* source on Hawaiiana today. His alma mater celebrates David Malo Day every year in April in recognition of his contributions to Hawaii.

Cross Prison Street. On the corner of Prison and Waihee is the:

20. Old Prison

The Hawaiians called the prison Hale Paahao (Stuck in Irons House). Sailors who refused to return to their boats at sunset used to be arrested and taken to the old fort). In 1851, however, the fort physician told the government that sleeping on the ground at night made the prisoners ill, costing the government quite a bit of money to treat them so the Kingdom of Hawaii used the prisoners to build a prison from the coral block of the old fort. Most prisoners here had terms of a year or less (those with longer terms were shipped off to Honolulu) and were convicted of crimes like deserting ship, being drunk, or working on Sunday. Today, the grounds of the prison have a much more congenial atmosphere and are rented out to community groups for parties.

Continue down Waihee Street, just past Waianae Place, to the small:

21. Episcopal Cemetery

This burial ground tells another story in Hawaii's history. During the reign of King Kamehameha IV, his wife, Queen Emma, formed close ties with British royalty. She encouraged Hawaiians to join the Anglican Church after asking the Archbishop of Canterbury to form a church in Hawaii. This cemetery contains the burial sites of many of those early Anglicans.

Next door is:

22. Hale Aloha

This "house of love" was built in 1858 by Hawaiians in "commemoration of God's causing Lahaina to escape the smallpox," while it decimated Oahu in 1853, carrying off 5,000 to 6,000 souls. The building served as a church and school until the turn of the 20th century, when it fell into disrepair. It is no longer standing, but artifacts remain.

Turn left onto Hale Street and then right onto Luakini Street to the:

23. Buddhist Church

This green wooden Shingon Buddhist temple is very typical of myriad Buddhist churches that sprang up all over the island when the Japanese laborers were brought to work in the sugar-cane fields.

Some of the churches were little more than elaborate false "temple" fronts on existing buildings.

On the side of Village Galleries, on the corner of Luakini and Dickenson streets, is the historical marker for:

24. Luakini Street

"Luakini" translates as a *heiau* (temple) where the ruling chiefs prayed and where human sacrifices were made. This street received its unforgettable name after serving as the route for the funeral procession of Princess Harriet Nahienaena, sister of kings Kamehameha II and III. The princess was a victim of the rapid changes in Hawaiian culture. A convert to Protestantism, she had fallen in love with her brother, Kamehameha III. Just 20 years earlier, their relationship would have been nurtured in order to preserve the purity of the royal bloodlines. The missionaries, however, frowned on brother and sister marrying. In August 1836, the couple had a son, who lived only a few short hours. Nahienaena never recovered and died in December of that same year (the king was said to mourn her death for years, frequently visiting her grave at the Waihee Cemetery). The route of her funeral procession through the breadfruit and koa trees to the cemetery became known as "Luakini," in reference to the gods "sacrificing" the beloved princess.

Turn left on Dickenson and walk down to Front Street, where you'll be back at the starting point.

25. Winding Down

Ready for some refreshment after your stroll? Head to Maui Swiss Cafe, 640 Front St. (tel. 808/661-6776), for tropical smoothies, great espresso, and affordable snacks. Sit in the funky garden area, or get your drink to go and wander over to the sea wall to watch the surfers.

Driving Tours

The Scenic Route from West Maui to Central or Upcountry Maui: The Kahekili Highway

The usual road from west Maui to Wailuku is the Honoapiilani Highway (Hwy. 30), which runs along the coast and then turns inland at Maalaea. But those in search of a back-to-nature driving experience should go the other way, along the Kahekili Highway (Hwy. 340). (*Highway* is a bit of a euphemism for this paved but somewhat precarious narrow road; check your rental-car agreement before you head out some companies don't allow their cars on this road. If it is raining or has been raining, skip this road due to mud and rock slides.) The road is named after the great chief Kahekili, who built houses from the skulls of his enemies.

You'll start out on the Honoapiilani Highway (Hwy. 30), which becomes the Kahekili Highway (Hwy. 340) after Honokohau, at the northernmost tip of the island. Around this point are Honolua Bay and Mokuleia Bay, which have been designated as Marine Life Conservation Areas (the taking of fish, shells, or anything else is prohibited).

From this point, the quality of the road deteriorates, and you may share the way with roosters, goats, cows, and dogs. The narrow road weaves along for the next 20 miles, following an ancient Hawaiian coastal footpath and showing you the true wild nature of Maui. These are photo opportunities from heaven: steep ravines, rolling pastoral hills, tumbling waterfalls, exploding blowholes, crashing surf, jagged lava coastlines, and a tiny Hawaiian village straight off a postcard.

Just before mile marker 20, look for a small turnoff on the mauka (mow-kah, meaning toward the mountain) side of the road, just before the guardrail starts. Park here and walk across the road, and on your left you'll see a spouting blowhole. In winter, this is an excellent spot to look for whales.

About 3 miles farther along the road, you'll come to a wide turnoff providing a great photo op: a view of the jagged coastline down to the crashing surf.

Less than half a mile farther along, just before mile marker 16, look for the POHAKU KANI sign, marking the huge, 6*6-foot bell-shaped stone. To "ring" the bell, look on the side facing Kahakuloa for the deep indentations, and strike the stone with another rock.

Along the route, nestled in a crevice between two steep hills, is the picturesque village of Kahakuloa (The Tall Hau Tree), with a dozen weather-worn houses, a church with a red-tile roof, and vivid green taro patches. From the northern side of the village, you can look back at the great view of Kahakuloa, the dark boulder beach, and the 636-foot Kahakuloa Head rising in the background.

At various points along the drive are artists' studios nestled into the cliffs and hills. One noteworthy stop is the Kaukini Gallery, located on Kahekili Hwy in Wailuku (808) 244-3371; www.kaukinigallery.com) which features work by more than two dozen local artists, with lots of gifts and crafts to buy in all price ranges. (You may also want to stop here to use one of the few restrooms along the drive.)

When you're approaching Wailuku, stop at the Halekii and Pihanakalani Heiau(www.mauimuseum.org/heiau.html) which visitors rarely see. To get here from Wailuku, turn north from Main Street onto Market Street. Turn right onto Mill Street and follow it until it ends; then make a left on Lower Main Street. Follow Lower Main until it ends at Waiehu Beach Road (Hwy. 340) and turn left. Turn left on Kuhio Street and again at the first left onto Hea Place, and drive through the gates and look for the Hawaii Visitors Bureau marker.

These two *heiau,* built in 1240 from stones carried up from the Iao Stream below, sit on a hill with a commanding view of central Maui and Haleakala. Kahekili, the last chief of Maui, lived here. After the bloody battle at Iao Stream, Kamehameha I reportedly came to the temple here to pay homage to the war god, Ku, with a human sacrifice. Halekii (House of Images) is made of stone walls with a flat grassy top, whereas Pihanakalani (Gathering Place of Supernatural Beings) is a pyramid-shaped mount of stones. If you sit quietly nearby (never walk on any *heiau* it's considered disrespectful), you'll see that the view alone explains why this spot was chosen.

The Road to Hana

Top down, sunscreen on, radio tuned to a little Hawaiian music on a Maui morning: It's time to head out to Hana along the Hana Highway (Hwy. 36), a wiggle of a road that runs along Maui's northeastern shore. The drive takes at least 3 hours from Lahaina or Kihei but plan to take all day. Going to Hana is about the journey, not the destination.

There are wilder roads, steeper roads, and more dangerous roads, but in all of Hawaii, no road is more celebrated than this one. It winds 50 miles past taro patches, magnificent seascapes, waterfall pools, botanical gardens, and verdant rainforests, and ends at one of Hawaii's most beautiful tropical places.

The outside world discovered the little village of Hana in 1926, when the narrow coastal road, carved by pickax-wielding convicts, opened. The mud-and-gravel road, often subject to landslides and washouts, was paved in 1962, when tourist traffic began to increase; now more than 1,000 cars traverse the road each day, according to storekeeper Harry Hasegawa. That equals about 500,000 people a year, which is way too many. Go at the wrong time, and you'll be stuck in a bumper-to-bumper rental-car parade peak traffic hours are midmorning and midafternoon year-round, especially on weekends.

In the rush to "do" Hana in a day, most visitors spin around town in 10 minutes flat and wonder what all the fuss is about. It takes time to take in Hana, play in the waterfalls, sniff the tropical flowers, hike to bamboo forests, and marvel at the spectacular scenery; stay overnight if you can.

However, if you really must do the Hana Highway in a day, go just before sunrise and return after sunset: On a full-moon night, the sea and the waterfalls glow in soft white light, with mysterious shadows appearing in the jungle. And you'll have the road almost to yourself on the way back.

Tips: Forget your mainland road manners. Practice aloha. Give way at one-lane bridges, wave at oncoming motorists, and let the big guys in 4*4s have the right of way it's just common sense, brah. If the guy behind you blinks his lights, let him pass. And don't honk your horn in Hawaii, it's considered rude.

The Journey Begins in Paia Before you even start out, fill up your gas tank. Gas in Paia is expensive (even by Maui standards), and it's the last place for gas until you get to Hana, some 42 miles, 54 bridges, and 600 hairpin turns down the road.

The former plantation village of Paia was once a thriving sugar-mill town. The mill is still here, but the population shifted to Kahului in the 1950s when subdivisions opened there, leaving Paia to shrivel up and die. But the town refused to give up and has proven its ability to adapt to the times. Now chic eateries and trendy shops stand next door to the mom-and-pop establishments that have been serving generations of Paia customers.

Plan to be here early, around 7am, when Charley's, 142 Hana Hwy. (tel. 808/579-9453), opens. Enjoy a big, hearty breakfast for a reasonable price.

After you leave Paia, just before the bend in the road, you'll pass the Kuau Mart on your left; a small general store, it's the only reminder of the sugar-plantation community of Kuau. The road then bends into an S-turn; in the middle of the S is the entrance to Mama's Fish House, marked by a restored boat with Mama's logo on the side. Just past the truck on the ocean side is the entrance to Mama's parking lot and adjacent small sandy cove in front of the restaurant. It's not good for swimming ocean access is over very slippery rocks into strong surf but the beach is a great place to sit and soak up some sun.

Windsurfing Mecca A mile from Mama's, just before mile marker 9, is a place known around the world as one of the greatest windsurfing spots on the planet, Hookipa Beach Park. Hookipa (Hospitality) is where the top-ranked windsurfers come to test themselves against the forces of nature: thunderous surf and forceful wind. World-championship contests are held here, but on nearly every windy afternoon (the board surfers have the waves in the morning), you can watch dozens of windsurfers twirling and dancing in the wind like colorful butterflies. To watch the windsurfers, do not stop on the highway, but go past the park and turn left at the entrance on the far side of the beach. You can either park on the high grassy bluff or drive down to the sandy beach and park alongside the pavilion. Facilities include restrooms, a shower, picnic tables, and a barbecue area.

Into the Country Past Hookipa Beach, the road winds down into Maliko (Budding) Gulch at mile marker 10. At the bottom of the gulch, look for the road on your right, which will take you out to Maliko Bay. Take the first right, which goes under the bridge and past a rodeo arena (scene of competitions by the Maliko Roping Club in summer) and on to the rocky beach. There are no facilities here except a boat-launch ramp. In the 1940s, Maliko had a thriving community at the mouth of the bay, but its residents rebuilt farther inland after a tsunami wiped it out. The bay may not look that special, but if the surf is up, it's a great place to watch the waves.

Back on the Hana Highway, as you leave Maliko Gulch, around mile marker 11, you'll pass through the rural area of Haiku, where you'll see banana patches, cane grass blowing in the wind, and forests of guava trees, avocados, kukui trees, palms, and Christmas berry. Just before mile marker 15 is the Maui-Grown Market and Deli(tel. 808/572-1693), a good stop for drinks or snacks for the ride.

Jaws If it's winter and the waves are up (like 60 ft. or so), here's your chance to watch tow-in surfing off Pauwela Point at an area known as Jaws (because the waves will chew you up), where expert tow-in surfers (who use a personal watercraft to pull a surfer into waves that are bigger than what could be caught by traditional paddling) battle the mammoth waves. To get here, make a small detour off the Hana Highway by turning left at Hahana Road, between mile markers 13 and 14. After the paved road ends, the dirt road is private property (Maui Land & Pine), so you may have to hike in about a mile and a half to get close to the ocean. Practice aloha, do not park in the pineapple fields, and do not pick or even touch the pineapples. Be very careful along the oceanside cliffs.

At mile marker 16, the curves begin, one right after another. Slow down and enjoy the view of bucolic rolling hills, mango trees, and vibrant ferns. After mile marker 16, the road is still called the Hana Highway, but the number changes from Hwy. 36 to Hwy. 360, and the mile markers go back to 0.

A Great Plunge Along the Way A dip in a waterfall pool is everybody's tropical-island fantasy. A great place to stop is Twin Falls, at mile marker 2. Just before the wide, concrete bridge, pull over on the mountain side and park. There is a NO TRESPASSING sign on the gate.

Although you will see several cars parked in the area and a steady line of people going up to the falls, be aware that this is private property and trespassing is illegal in Hawaii. If you decide that you want to risk it, you will walk about 3 to 5 minutes to the waterfall and pool, or continue on another 10 to 15 minutes to the second, larger waterfall and pool (don't go in if it has been raining).

Hidden Huelo Just before mile marker 4 on a blind curve, look for a double row of mailboxes on the left side by a pay phone. Down the road lies a hidden Hawaii of an earlier time, where an indescribable sense of serenity prevails. Hemmed in by Waipo and Hoalua bays is the remote community of Huelo, which means "tail end, last." This fertile area once supported a population of 75,000; today only a few hundred live among the scattered homes here, where a handful of B&Bs and exquisite vacation rentals cater to a trickle of travelers.

The only reason Huelo is even marked is the historic 1853 Kaulanapueo Church.Reminiscent of New England architecture, this coral-and-cement church, topped with a plantation-green steeple and a gray tin roof, is still in use, although services are held just once or twice a month. It still has the same austere interior of 1853: straight-backed benches, a no-nonsense platform for the minister, and no distractions on the walls to tempt you from paying attention to the sermon. Next to the church is a small graveyard, a personal history of this village in concrete and stone.

Koolau Forest Reserve After Huelo, the vegetation seems more lush, as though Mother Nature had poured Miracle-Gro on everything. This is the edge of the Koolau Forest Reserve. Koolau means "windward," and this certainly is one of the greatest examples of a lush windward area: The coastline here gets about 60 to 80 inches of rain a year, as well as runoff from the 200 to 300 inches that falls from farther up the mountain. You'll see trees laden with guavas, as well as mangoes, java plums, and avocados the size of softballs. The spiny, long-leafed plants are hala trees, which the Hawaiians used for weaving baskets, mats, and even canoe sails.

From here on out, there's a waterfall (and a one-lane bridge) around nearly every turn in the road, so drive slowly and be prepared to stop and yield to oncoming cars.

Dangerous Curves About 1/2 mile after mile marker 6, there's a sharp U-curve in the road, going uphill. The road is practically one-lane here, with a brick wall on one side and virtually no maneuvering room. Sound your horn at the start of the U-curve to let approaching cars know you're coming. Take this curve, as well as the few more coming up in the next several miles, very slowly.

Just before mile marker 7 is a forest of waving bamboo. The sight is so spectacular that drivers are often tempted to take their eyes off the road. Be very cautious. Wait until just after mile marker 7, at the Kaaiea (Breathtaking View) Bridge and stream below, to pull over and take a closer look at the hand-hewn stone walls. Then turn around to see the vista of bamboo.

A Great Family Hike At mile marker 9, there's a small state wayside area with restrooms, picnic tables, and a barbecue area. The sign says KOOLAU FOREST RESERVE, but the real attraction here is the Waikamoi Ridge Trail, a great family hike that wanders on a clearly marked path, has a very gentle slope (easy enough for toddlers and grandparents) and scenic vistas, lots of interesting vegetation (which is marked with signs). The .75 mile loop is just the right amount of time to stretch your legs and be ready to get back in the car and head to Hana.

Safety Warning I used to recommend another waterfall, Puohokamoa Falls, at mile marker 11, but not anymore. Unfortunately, what was once a great thing has been overrun by hordes of not-so-polite tourists. You will see cars parking on the already dangerous, barely two-lane Hana Highway 1/2 mile before the waterfall. Slow down after mile marker 10. As you get close to mile marker 11, the highway becomes a congested one-lane road due to visitors parking on this narrow stretch. Don't add to the congestion by trying to park: There are plenty of other great waterfalls; just drive slowly and safely through this area.

Can't-Miss Photo Ops Just past mile marker 12 is the Kaumahina State Wayside Park (kaumahina means "moon rise"). This is not only a good pit stop (restrooms are available) and a wonderful place for a picnic (with tables and a barbecue area), but also a great vista point. The view of the rugged coastline makes an excellent shot you can see all the way down to the jutting Keanae Peninsula.

Another mile and a couple of bends in the road, and you'll enter the Honomanu Valley, with its beautiful bay. To get to the Honomanu Bay County Beach Park, look for the turnoff on your left, just after mile marker 14, located at a point in the road where you begin your ascent up the other side of the valley. The rutted dirt-and-cinder road takes you down to the rocky black-sand beach. There are no facilities here. Because of the strong rip currents offshore, swimming is best in the stream inland from the ocean. You'll consider the drive down worthwhile as you stand on the beach, well away from the ocean, and turn to look back on the steep cliffs covered with vegetation.

Maui's Botanical World Farther along the winding road, between mile markers 16 and 17, is a cluster of bunkhouses composing the YMCA Camp Keanae. A 1/4-mile down is the Keanae Arboretum, where the region's botany is divided into three parts: native forest, introduced forest, and traditional Hawaiian plants, food, and medicine. You can swim in the pools of Piinaau Stream, or press on along a mile-long trail into Keanae Valley, where a lovely tropical rainforest waits at the end.

Keanae Peninsula The old Hawaiian village of Keanae (The Mullet) stands out against the Pacific like a place time forgot. Here, on an old lava flow graced by an 1860 stone church and swaying palms, is one of the last coastal enclaves of native Hawaiians. They still grow taro in patches and pound it into poi, the staple of the old Hawaiian diet. And they still pluck opihi (limpet) from tide pools along the jagged coast and cast throw nets at schools of fish.

The turnoff to the Keanae Peninsula is on the left, just after the arboretum. The road passes by farms as it hugs the peninsula. Where the road bends, there's a small beach where fishermen gather to catch dinner. A 1/4 mile farther is the Keanae Congregational Church (tel. 808/248-8040), built in 1860 of lava rocks and coral mortar, standing in stark contrast to the green fields surrounding it. Beside the church is a small beachfront park, with false kamani trees against a backdrop of black lava and a roiling turquoise sea.

To experience untouched Hawaii, follow the road until it ends. Park by the white fence and take the short 5-minute walk along the shoreline over the black lava. Continue along the footpath through the tall California grass to the black rocky beach, separating the freshwater stream, Pinaau, which winds back into the Keanae Peninsula, nearly cutting it off from the rest of Maui. This is an excellent place for a picnic and a swim in the cool waters of the stream. There are no facilities here, so be sure you carry everything out with you and use restrooms before you arrive. As you make your way back, notice the white PVC pipes sticking out of the rocks they're fishing-pole holders for fishermen, usually hoping to catch ulua.

Another Photo Op: Keanae Lookout Just past mile marker 17 is a wide spot on the ocean side of the road, where you can see the entire Keanae Peninsula's checkerboard pattern of green taro fields and its ocean boundary etched in black lava. Keanae was the result of a postscript eruption of Haleakala, which flowed through the Koolau Gap and down Keanae Valley and added this geological punctuation to the rugged coastline.

Fruit and Flower Stands Around mile marker 18, the road widens; you'll start to see numerous small stands selling fruit or flowers. Many of these stands work on the honor system: You leave your money in the basket and select your purchase. I recommend stopping at Uncle Harry's, which you'll find just after the Keanae School around mile marker 18. His family sells a variety of fruits and juices here Monday through Saturday from 9am to 4pm.

Wailua Just after Uncle Harry's, look for Wailua Road on the left. This will take you through the hamlet of homes and churches of Wailua, which also contains a shrine depicting what the community calls a "miracle." Behind the pink St. Gabriel's Church is the smaller, blue-and-white Coral Miracle Church, home of the Our Lady of Fatima Shrine. According to legend, in 1860 the men of this village were building a church by diving for coral to make the stone. But the coral offshore was in deep water and the men could only come up with a few pieces at a time, making the construction of the church an arduous project. A freak storm hit the area and deposited the coral from the deep on a nearby beach. The Hawaiians gathered what they needed and completed the church. After the church was completed, another freak storm hit the area and swept all the remaining coral on the beach back out to sea.

If you look back at Haleakala from here, on your left you can see the spectacular, near-vertical Waikani Falls. On the remainder of the dead-end road is an eclectic collection of old and modern homes. Turning around at the road's end is very difficult, so I suggest you just turn around at the church and head back for the Hana Highway.

Back on the Hana Highway, just before mile marker 19, is the Wailua Valley State Wayside Park (wailua means "two waters"), on the right side of the road. Climb up the stairs for a view of the Keanae Valley, waterfalls, and Wailua Peninsula. On a really clear day, you can see up the mountain to the Koolau Gap.

For a better view of the Wailua Peninsula, continue down the road about 1/4 mile. There's a pull-off area with parking on the ocean side.

Puaa Kaa State Wayside Park You'll hear this park long before you see it, about halfway between mile markers 22 and 23. The sound of waterfalls provides the background music for this small park area with restrooms, a phone, and a picnic area. In fact, puaa kaa translates as "open laughter." There's a well-marked path to the falls and to a swimming hole. Ginger plants are everywhere: Pick some flowers and put them in your car so that you can travel with that sweet smell.

Old Nahiku Just after mile marker 25 is a narrow 3-mile road leading from the highway, at about 1,000 feet elevation, down to sea level and to the remains of the old Hawaiian community of Nahiku. At one time this was a thriving village of thousands; today, the population has dwindled to fewer than 100 including a few Hawaiian families, but mostly extremely wealthy mainland residents who jet in for a few weeks at a time to their luxurious vacation homes. At the turn of the 20th century, this site saw brief commercial activity as home of the Nahiku Rubber Co., the only commercial rubber plantation in the United States. You can still see rubber trees along Nahiku Road. However, the amount of rainfall, coupled with the damp conditions, could not support the commercial crop; the plantation closed in 1912, and Nahiku was forgotten until the 1980s, when multimillionaires "discovered" the remote and stunningly beautiful area.

At the end of the road, you can see the remains of the old wharf from the rubber-plantation days. Local residents come down here to shoreline fish; there's a small picnic area off to the side. Dolphins are frequently seen in the bay.

Hana Airport After mile marker 31, a small sign points to the Hana Airport, down Alalele Road on the left. Commuter airline Pacific Wings (tel. 888/575-4546;www.pacificwings.com) offers four flights daily to and from Hana (from Kahului), with connecting flights from Kahului and traveling on to Honolulu. Be warned: There is no public transportation in Hana. Car rentals are available through Kihei Rent A Car(tel. 800/251-5288 or 808/879-7257; www.KiheiRentACar.com).

Waianapanapa State Park At mile marker 32, just on the outskirts of Hana, shiny black-sand Waianapanapa Beach appears like a vivid dream, with bright-green jungle foliage on three sides and cobalt-blue water lapping at its feet. The 120-acre park on an ancient lava flow includes sea cliffs, lava tubes, arches, and the beach, plus 12 cabins, tent camping, picnic pavilions, restrooms, showers, drinking water, and hiking trails.

Important Information

The Best Luxury Hotels

Hyatt Regency Maui Resort & Spa (tel. **800/233-1234** or 808/661-1234; www.maui.hyatt.com): Spagoers will love Hawaii's first oceanfront spa. The 806 rooms of this fantasy resort, spread out among three towers, have very comfortable separate sitting areas and private lanai with eye-popping views. This huge place covers some 40 acres; even if you don't stay here, you might want to walk through the expansive tree-filled atrium and the parklike grounds.

Kaanapali Alii (tel. **800/642-6284** or 808/661-3330; www.kaanapali-alii.com): The height of luxury, these oceanfront condominium units (right on Kaanapali Beach) combine all the amenities of a luxury hotel (including a 24-hr. front desk) with the convenience of a condominium. The beachside recreation area includes a swimming pool, a separate children's pool, a whirlpool, gas barbecue grills and picnic areas, exercise rooms, saunas, and tennis courts.

Sheraton Maui Resort (tel. **866/716-8109** or **808/661-0031**; www.sheraton-maui.com): Offering the best location on Kaanapali Beach, recent renovations, and a great hassle-free experience, the Sheraton is my pick of Kaanapali hotels. This is the place for travelers who just want to arrive, have everything ready for them, and get on with their vacation. (Sheraton has a "no-hassle" check-in: The valet takes you and your luggage straight to your room, which means no time wasted standing in line at registration.)

Ritz-Carlton Kapalua (tel. **800/262-8440** or **808/669-6200**; www.ritzcarlton.com): With its great location, style, and loads of hospitality, this is the best Ritz anywhere. Situated on the coast below the picturesque West Maui Mountains, this grand, breezy hotel overlooks the Pacific Ocean and Molokai across the channel. The natural setting, on an old coastal pineapple plantation, is the picture of tranquillity. The service is legendary, the golf courses are daunting, and the nearby beaches are perfect for snorkeling, diving, and just relaxing.

The Fairmont Kea Lani Maui (tel. **800/659-4100** or 808/875-4100; www.fairmont.com/kealani): This all-suite luxury hotel in Wailea has 840-square-foot suites featuring kitchenettes with microwaves and coffeemakers, living rooms with high-tech media centers and pullout sofa beds (great if you have the kids in tow), marble wet bars, and spacious bedrooms. The oversize marble bathrooms have separate showers big enough for a party. Large lanai off the bedrooms and living rooms overlook the pools and lawns, with views that sweep right down to the white-sand beach.

Hotel Hana-Maui (tel. **800/321-HANA** [4262] or 808/248-8211; www.hotelhanamaui.com): Picture Shangri-La, Hawaiian style: 66 acres rolling down to the sea in a remote Hawaiian village, with two pools and access to one of the best beaches in Hana. This is the atmosphere, the landscape, and the culture of old Hawaii set in the latest accommodations of the 21st century. A white-sand beach just a 5-minute shuttle ride away, a top-notch wellness center, and numerous activities (horseback riding, mountain biking, tennis, pitch-and-putt golf) all add up to make this one of the top resorts in the state.

Grand Wailea Resort Hotel & Spa (tel. **800/888-6100** or 808/875-1234; www.grandwailea.com): There's nothing subtle or understated about it, but many travelers adore this over-the-top fantasy resort. It has 10,000 tropical plants in the lobby; a fabulous pool with slides, waterfalls, and rapids; Hawaii's largest spa; plush oceanview rooms; and a superb location on a gorgeous stretch of beach.

Four Seasons Resort Maui at Wailea (tel. **800/334-MAUI** [6284] or 808/874-8000; www.fourseasons.com/maui): This is the ultimate beach hotel for latter-day royals, offering excellent cuisine, spacious rooms, gracious service, and Wailea Beach one of Maui's best gold-sand beaches right outside the front door. Every room has at least a partial ocean view from a private lanai. The luxury suites are as big as some Honolulu condos and full of marble and deluxe appointments.

The Best Mid-Range Hotels

The Plantation Inn (tel. **800/433-6815** or 808/667-9225; www.theplantationinn.com): Attention, romance-seeking couples: You need look no further. This charming Lahaina hotel looks like it's been here 100 years or more, but looks can be deceiving. The Victorian-style inn is actually of 1990s vintage an artful deception. The rooms are romantic to the max, tastefully done with period furniture, hardwood floors, stained glass, ceiling fans, and four-poster canopy beds. The rooms wrap around the large pool and deck; also on-site are a spa and an elegant pavilion lounge, where breakfast is served, all starting at $159 double.

Lahaina Inn

(tel. **800/669-3444** or 808/661-0577; www.lahainainn.com): If the romance of historic Lahaina catches your fancy, a stay here will really complete the experience. Built in 1938 as a general store, this building has been restored as a charming, antiques-filled inn right in the heart of town, with room rates as low as $150. Downstairs, you'll find one of Hawaii's most popular storefront bistros, Lahaina Grill.

Kahana Sunset

(tel. **800/669-1488** or 808/669-8011; www.kahanasunset.com): This is a great choice for families, featuring a series of wooden condo units stair-stepping down the side of a hill to a postcard-perfect white-sand beach. The units feature full kitchens, washer/dryers, large lanai with terrific views, and sleeper sofas (starting at $150 for up to four people).

Punahoa Beach Apartments (tel. **800/564-4380** or 808/879-2720; www.punahoabeach.com): This small ocean-side Kihei condo complex is hidden on a quiet side street; the grassy lawn out front rolls about 50 feet down to the beach. You'll find great snorkeling just offshore and a popular surfing spot next door, with shopping and restaurants all within walking distance. Every well-decorated unit features a lanai with fabulous ocean views; rates start at $132 double for a studio.

Best Dining Bets

A Saigon Cafe (tel. **808/243-9560**): Jennifer Nguyen's unmarked dining room in an odd corner of Wailuku is always packed, a tribute to her clean, crisp Vietnamese cuisine and the Maui grapevine. Grab a round of rice paper and wrap your own Vietnamese "burrito" of tofu, noodles, and vegetables.

A.K.'s Café (tel. **808/244-8774;** www.akscafe.com): Chef Elaine Rothermel has a winner with this tiny cafe in the industrial district of Wailuku. It may be slightly off the tourist path, and the decor isn't much to look at, but it is well worth the effort to find this delicious eatery, with creative cuisine coming out of the kitchen most of it healthy. Prices are so eye-poppingly cheap, you might find yourself wandering back here again during your vacation.

David Paul's Island Grill

(tel. **808/662-3000;** www.davidpaulsislandgrill.com): One of Hawaii's top chefs, David Paul, opened a restaurant in Lahaina, introducing a combination of American and island-style cuisine that draws heavily on local products. He dubbed this "new island cooking."

Gerard's (tel. 808/661-8939; www.gerardsmaui.com): Proving that French is fabulous, particularly in the land of sushi and sashimi, Gerard Reversade is the Gallic gastronome who delivers ecstasy with every bite. From the rack of lamb to the spinach salad and oyster mushrooms in puff pastry, every meal is memorable. The fairy lights on the veranda in the balmy outdoor Lahaina setting are the icing on the gâteau.

Mala Ocean Tavern (tel. 808/667-9394; www.malaoceantavern.com): Perched right on the ocean, this tiny "tavern" is the brainchild of Mark and Judy Ellman, owners of Maui Tacos and Penne Pasta Café. They use healthy, organically grown food and fresh fish to make intriguing dishes. The atmosphere could not be more enticing, with just a handful of tables out on the oceanfront lanai and several more tables in the warmly decorated interior. The staff is helpful and efficient, and the food is outstanding.

Son'z Maui at Swan Court
(tel. 808/667-4506; www.tristarrestaurants.com): For 30 years, the Swan Court was *the* dining experience at the Hyatt Regency Maui Resort, and under Tri-Star Restaurant Group, it's even better. The

restaurant already had perhaps the most romantic location in Maui, overlooking a man-made lagoon with white and black swans swimming by and the rolling surf of the Pacific in the distance. The culinary team's creative dishes, coupled with fresh local ingredients, have made it a must for every Maui visitor.

Roy's Kahana Bar & Grill

(tel. **808/669-6999;** www.roysrestaurant.com): This restaurant bustles with young, hip servers impeccably trained to deliver blackened ahi or perfectly seared lemon grass *shutome* (broadbill swordfish) hot to your table, in rooms that sizzle with cross-cultural tastings.

Pineapple Grill (tel. **808/669-9600;** www.pineapplekapalua.com): If you only had a single night to eat on the island, I'd send you here. In fact, if you eat here at the beginning of your Maui trip, you might end up coming back! Chef Ryan Luckey is a genius at turning fresh local ingredients into culinary masterpieces, such as the Maui-style seafood paella with Portuguese sausage and Kula herbs.

Plantation House Restaurant (tel. **808/669-6299;**www.theplantationhouse.com): Plantation House features teak tables, a fireplace, open sides, mountain and ocean views, and Chef Alex Stanislaw's love for Mediterranean flavors and preparations. It's a friendly, comfortable restaurant with great food, including sublime eggs Mediterranean at breakfast and polenta, crab cakes, fish, pork tenderloin, filet mignon, and other delights at dinner. The ambience is superb.

Ko

(tell **808/875-4100;**www.fairmont.com/kealani/GuestServices/Restaurants/Ko.htm): The concept behind this successful restaurant in the Fairmont Kea Lani is pure genius taking the various ethnic cuisine from Maui's old plantation days (Hawaiian, Filipino, Portuguese, Korean, Puerto Rican, and European) and cooking them up in a gourmet fashion. There are some wonderful taste treats you are going to find only here, so don't miss them: ahi (which is tuna) "on the rocks," where the server brings you chunks of fresh ahi and you cook them on hot *ishiyaki* stone to the desired doneness (from barely seared on the outside to fully cooked). Or Filipino *lumpia* (a sort of spring roll with green papaya, shrimp, and pork [or chicken and mushroom] that you dip into a spicy sauce).

Sansei Seafood Restaurant & Sushi Bar (tel. **808/669-6286** in Kapalua, 879-0004 in Kihei; www.sanseihawaii.com): Relentlessly popular, Sansei serves sushi and then some: hand rolls warm and cold, *udon* and ramen, and the signature Asian rock-shrimp cake with the oh-so-complex lime-chili butter and cilantro pesto. This place is flavor central simplicity is not its strong suit, so be prepared for some busy tasting.

Gannon's (tel. **808/875-8080;** www.gannonsrestaurant.com): Another fabulous restaurant by award-winning-chef Bev Gannon, who has taken over the former Sea Watch restaurant, perched high on a hill, overlooking the Wailea Golf Course and the spectacular ocean view with Molokini in the distance, and produces meals with magic.

Joe's (tel. **808/875-7767;** www.bevgannonrestaurants.com): The impressive view here spans the Wailea golf course, tennis courts, ocean, and Haleakala a worthy setting for Beverly Gannon's style of American home cooking with a regional twist. The hearty staples include excellent mashed potatoes, lobster, fresh fish, and filet mignon, but the meatloaf (a whole loaf, like Mom used to make) upstages them all.

Haliimaile General Store
(tel. **808/572-2666;**www.bevgannonrestaurants.com/haliimaile): Bev Gannon, one of the 12 original Hawaii Regional Cuisine chefs, is still going strong at her foodie haven in the pineapple fields. You'll dine at tables set on old wood floors under high ceilings. The food, a blend of eclectic American with ethnic touches, bridges Hawaii and Gannon's Texas roots to put an innovative spin on Hawaii Regional Cuisine.

Examples include sashimi napoleon and the house salad island greens with mandarin oranges, onions, toasted walnuts, and blue-cheese crumble.

Moana Bakery & Cafe (tel. **808/579-9999;** www.moanacafe.com): In the unlikely location of Paia, the Moana gets high marks for its stylish concrete floors, high ceilings, booths and cafe tables, and fabulous food. Don Ritchey, formerly a chef at Haliimaile General Store, has created the perfect Paia eatery, a casual bakery/cafe that highlights his stellar skills. It may not look like much from the outside, but don't be fooled. This innovative eatery serves breakfast, lunch, and dinner and offers live entertainment at night.

Colleen's at the Cannery
(tel. **808/575-9211;** www.colleensinhaiku.com): Way, way, way off the beaten path lies this chic, fabulous find in the rural Haiku Cannery Marketplace. It's worth the drive to enjoy Colleen's fabulous culinary creations, such as wild-mushroom ravioli with sautéed Portobello mushrooms, tomatoes, herbs, and a roasted-pepper *coulis*.

Market Fresh Bistro (tel. **808/572-4877**): Attention foodies: Plan to eat dinner here at least once during your stay on Maui. Yes, it is a long drive from a resort area, and yes, parking is on the street and you may have to walk a block or two, but Chef Justin Pardo (formerly of the

Union Square Café, New York City and the Wailea Grand on Maui) is a culinary genius and he uses 90% local products and is having fun creating menus at this off-the-beaten-path restaurant, hidden in a minimall complex, behind the Makawao Steak House.

Old Lahaina Luau

(tel. **800/248-5828** or 808/667-1998; www.oldlahainaluau.com): It's not exactly a restaurant, but it's certainly an unforgettable dining experience. Maui's best luau serves top-quality food that's as much Pacific Rim as authentically Hawaiian, served from an open-air thatched structure. It's one-third entertainment, one-third good food, and one-third ambience.

The Best Shopping

Sandell (tel. **808/249-0234;** www.sandellmaui.com): Since the early 1970s, artist, illustrator, and cartoonist David Sandell has been commenting on Maui through his artwork. Don't miss the opportunity to stop by his shop in old Wailuku town and "talk story" with the talented artist, who watched Maui go from undiscovered to discovered. His work from original oils to prints to T-shirts makes excellent souvenirs to take home.

Bailey House Museum Shop

(tel. **808/244-3326;** www.mauimuseum.org): You can travel Hawaii and peruse its past with the assemblage of made-in-Hawaii items at this museum gift shop in Wailuku. Tropical preserves, Hawaiian music, pareu, prints by esteemed Hawaiian artists, cookbooks, hatbands, and magnificent wood bowls reflect a discerning standard of selection. Unequaled for Hawaiian treasures on Maui.

Brown-Kobayashi (tel. **808/242-0804**): At this quiet, tasteful, and elegant Asian shop in Wailuku, the selection of antiques and collectibles changes constantly but reflects an unwavering sense of gracious living. There are old and new European and Hawaiian objects, from koa furniture (which disappears fast) to lacquerware, Bakelite jewelry, Peking glass beads, and a few priceless pieces of antique ivory.

Village Galleries (tel. **808/661-4402** in Lahaina, 808/669-1800 in Kapalua; www.villagegalleriesmaui.com): Maui's oldest galleries have maintained high standards and the respect of a public that is increasingly impatient with clichéd island art. On exhibit are the finest contemporary Maui artists in all media, with a discerning selection of handcrafted jewelry. In Lahaina, the contemporary gallery has a larger selection of jewelry, ceramics, glass, and gift items, as well as paintings and prints.

Hui No'eau Visual Arts Center

(tel. **808/572-6560**; www.huinoeau.com): Half the experience is the center itself, one of Maui's historic treasures: a strikingly designed 1917 *kamaaina* (native-born, or old-timer) estate on 9 acres in Makawao; two of Maui's largest hybrid Cook and Norfolk pines; and an arts center with classes, exhibitions, and demonstrations. The gift shop is as memorable as the rest of it. You'll find one-of-a-kind works by local artists, from prints to jewelry and pottery.

Viewpoints Gallery

(tel. **808/572-5979**; www.viewpointsgallerymaui.com): I love this airy, well-designed Makawao gallery and its helpful staff, which complement the fine Maui art: paintings, sculpture, jewelry, prints, woods, and glass. This is Maui's only fine-arts cooperative, showcasing the work of dozens of local artists.

Hana Coast Gallery (tel. **808/248-8636**; www.hanacoast.com): This gallery is a good reason to go to Hana: It's an aesthetic and cultural experience that informs as it enlightens. Tucked away in the posh hideaway Hotel Hana-Maui, the 3,000-square-foot gallery is known for its high level of curatorship and commitment to the cultural art of

Hawaii. It's devoted entirely to Hawaiian artists, who display their sculptures, paintings, prints, feather work, stonework, and carvings

The Best Adventures

Branch out while you're in Maui. Do something you wouldn't normally do after all, you're on vacation. Some of the following adventures are a bit pricey, but these splurges are worth every penny.

Scuba Diving: You're in love with snorkeling and the chance to view the underwater world, but it's just not enough you want to get closer and see even more. Take an introductory scuba dive: After a brief lesson on how to use the diving equipment, you'll plunge into the deep to swim with the tropical fish and go eyeball to eyeball with other marine critters.

Skimming over the Ocean in a Kayak: Glide silently over the water, hearing only the sound of your paddle dipping beneath the surface. This is the way the early Hawaiians traveled along the coastline. You'll be eye level and up close and personal with the ocean and the coastline, exploring areas you can't get to any other way. Venture out on your own or go with an experienced guide either way, you won't be sorry.

Seeing the Stars from Inside a Volcanic Crater: Driving up to see the sunrise is a trip you'll never forget, but to *really* experience Haleakala, plan to hike in and spend the night. To get a feel for why the ancient Hawaiians considered this one of the most sacred places on the island, you simply have to wander into the heart of the dormant volcano, where you'll find some 27 miles of hiking trails, two camping sites, and three cabins.

Hiking to a Waterfall: There are waterfalls and then there are *waterfalls:* The magnificent 400-foot Waimoku Falls, in Oheo Gulch outside of Hana, are worth the long drive and the uphill hike you have to take to get there. The falls are surrounded by lush green ferns and wild orchids, and you can even stop to take a dip in the pool at the top of Makahiku Falls on the way.

Flying over the Remote West Maui Mountains: Your helicopter streaks low over razor-thin cliffs, then flutters past sparkling waterfalls and down into the canyons and valleys of the inaccessible West Maui Mountains. There's so much beauty to absorb that it all goes by in a rush. You'll never want to stop flying over this spectacular, surreal landscape and it's the only way to see the dazzling beauty of the prehistoric area of Maui.

Taking a Drive on the Wild Side: Mother Nature's wild side, that is on the Kahekili Highway on Maui's northeast coast. This back-to-nature experience will take you past ancient Hawaiian *heiau* (temples); along steep ravines; and by rolling pastures, tumbling waterfalls, exploding blowholes, crashing surf, and jagged lava coastlines. You'll wander through the tiny Hawaiian village of Kahakuloa and around the "head" of Maui to the Marine Life Conservation Area of Honolua-Mokuleia and on to the resort of Kapalua. You'll remember this adventure for years.

The Best Resorts & Spas

Spa Moana at the Hyatt Regency Maui Resort & Spa (tel. **800/233-1234** or 808/661-1234; www.maui.hyatt.com): The island's first oceanfront spa, this 20,000-square-foot facility offers an open-air exercise lanai, wet-treatment rooms, massage rooms, a relaxation lounge, sauna and steam rooms, a Roman pool illuminated by overhead skylights, and a duet treatment suite for couples.

Spa at the Ritz-Carlton Kapalua (tel. **800/262-8440** or 808/669-6200; www.ritzcarlton.com): Book a massage on the beach. The spa itself is welcoming and wonderful, but there is nothing like smelling the salt in the air and feeling the gentle caress of the wind in your hair while experiencing a true Hawaiian massage.

Spa Kea Lani at the Fairmont Kea Lani Maui (tel. **800/659-4100** or 808/875-4100; www.fairmont.com/kealani): This intimate, Art Deco boutique spa (just a little over 5,000 sq. ft., with nine treatment rooms) is the place for personal and private attention. The fitness center next door is open 24 hours (a rarity in Hawaiian resorts) with a personal trainer on duty some 14 hours a day.

Spa at the Four Seasons Resort Maui at Wailea (tel. **800/334-MAUI** [6284] or 808/874-8000; www.fourseasons.com/maui): Imagine the sound of the waves rolling on Wailea Beach as you are soothingly massaged in the privacy of your cabana, tucked in among the beachside foliage. This is the place to come to be absolutely spoiled. Yes, there's an excellent workout area and tons of great classes, but the specialty here is hedonistic indulgence.

Spa Grande at the Grand Wailea Resort Hotel & Spa (tel. **800/888-6100** or 808/875-1234; www.grandwailea.com): This is Hawaii's biggest spa, at 50,000 square feet and with 40 treatment rooms. The spa incorporates the best of the Old World (romantic ceiling murals, larger-than-life Roman-style sculptures, mammoth Greek columns, huge European tubs), the finest Eastern traditions (a full Japanese-style traditional bath and various exotic treatments from India), and the lure of the islands (tropical foliage, ancient Hawaiian treatments, and island products). It has everything from a top fitness center to a menu of classes and is constantly on the cutting edge of the latest trends.

vvvvvvv

The Best of Underwater Maui

An entirely different Maui greets anyone with a face mask, snorkel, and fins. Under the sea, you'll find schools of brilliant tropical fish, green sea turtles, quick-moving game fish, slack-jawed moray eels, and prehistoric-looking coral. It's a kaleidoscope of color and wonder.

Black Rock: This spot, located on Kaanapali Beach just off the Sheraton Maui Resort, is excellent for beginning snorkelers during the day and for scuba divers at night. Schools of fish congregate at the base of the rock and are so used to snorkelers that they go about their business as if no one was around. If you take the time to look closely at the crannies of the rock, you'll find lion fish in fairly shallow water. At night (when a few outfitters run night dives here), lobsters, Spanish dancers, and eels come out.

Olowalu: When the wind is blowing and the waves are crashing everywhere else, Olowalu, the small area 5 miles south of Lahaina, can be a scene of total calm perfect for snorkeling and diving. You'll find a good snorkeling area around mile marker 14. You might have to swim about 50 to 75 feet; when you get to the large field of finger coral in 10 to 15 feet of water, you're there. You'll see a turtle-cleaning station, where turtles line up to have small cleaner wrasses pick off small parasites. This is also a good spot to see crown-of-thorns starfish, puffer fish, and lots of juvenile fish.

Hawaiian Reef: Scuba divers love this area off the Kihei-Wailea coast because it has a good cross-section of topography and marine life typical of Hawaiian waters. Diving to depths of 85 feet, you'll see everything from lava formations and coral reef to sand and rubble, plus a diverse range of both shallow- and deepwater creatures."

Third Tank: Scuba divers looking for a photo opportunity will find it at this artificial reef, located off Makena Beach at 80 feet. This World War II tank acts like a fish magnet: Because it's the only large solid object in the area, any fish or invertebrate looking for a safe home comes here. Surrounding the tank is a cloak of schooling snappers and goatfish just waiting for a photographer with a wide-angle lens. It's small, but Third Tank is loaded with more marine life per square inch than any site off Maui."

Molokini: Shaped like a crescent moon, this islet's shallow concave side serves as a sheltering backstop against sea currents for tiny tropical fish; on its opposite side is a deepwater cliff inhabited by spiny lobsters, moray eels, and white-tipped sharks. Neophyte snorkelers report to the concave side; experienced scuba divers, the cliff side. Either way, the clear water and abundant marine life make this islet off the Makena coast one of Hawaii's most popular dive spots.

Ahihi-Kinau Natural Preserve: Fishing is strictly *kapu* (forbidden) in Ahihi Bay (at the end of the road in south Maui), and the fish seem to know it they're everywhere in this series of rocky coves and black-lava tide pools. The black, barren, lunarlike land stands in stark contrast to the green-blue water, which is home to a sparkling mosaic of tropical fish. Scuba divers might want to check out La Pérouse Pinnacle in the middle of La Pérouse Bay; clouds of damselfish and triggerfish will greet you on the surface.

The Best Beaches

D.T. Fleming Beach Park: This quiet, out-of-the-way beach, located north of the Ritz-Carlton hotel, starts at the 16th hole of the Kapalua Golf Course (Makaluapuna Point) and rolls around to the sea cliffs on the other side of the cove. Ironwood trees provide shade on the land side. Offshore, a shallow sandbar extends out to the edge of the surf. The waters are generally good for swimming and snorkeling, but sometimes, near the sea cliffs, the waves are big enough to suit body boarders and surfers.

Kapalua Beach: On an island of many great beaches, this one takes the prize. A golden crescent with swaying palms protected from strong winds and currents by two outstretched lava-rock promontories, Kapalua has calm waters that are perfect for snorkeling, swimming, and kayaking. Even though it borders the Kapalua Resort, the beach is long enough for everyone to enjoy. Facilities include showers, restrooms, and lifeguards.

Kaanapali Beach: Four-mile-long Kaanapali stands out as one of Maui's best beaches, with grainy gold sand as far as the eye can see. Most of the beach parallels the sea channel, and a paved beach walk links hotels and condos, open-air restaurants, and the Whalers Village shopping center. Summertime swimming is excellent. The best snorkeling is around Black Rock, in front of the Sheraton; the water is clear, calm, and populated with brilliant tropical fish.

Wailea Beach: This is the best gold-sand, crescent-shaped beach on Maui's sun-baked southwestern coast. One of five beaches within Wailea Resort, Wailea Beach is big, wide, and protected on both sides by black-lava points. It serves as the front yard for the Four Seasons Resort, Maui's most elegant hotel, and the Grand Wailea Resort, its most outrageous. From the beach, the view out to sea is magnificent, framed by neighboring Kahoolawe and Lanai and the tiny crescent of Molokini. The clear waters tumble to shore in waves just the right size for gentle riding, with or without a board. All the beaches on the west and south coasts are great for spotting whales, but Wailea, with its fairly flat sandy beach that gently slopes down to the ocean, provides exceptionally good whale-watching from shore in season (Dec-Apr).

Maluaka Beach (Makena Beach): On the southern end of Maui's resort coast, development falls off dramatically, leaving a wild, dry countryside punctuated by green kiawe trees. This wide, palm-fringed crescent of golden sand is set between two black-lava points and bounded by big sand dunes topped by a grassy knoll. Makena can be perfect for swimming when it's flat and placid, but it can also offer excellent bodysurfing when the waves come rolling in. Molokini and Kahoolawe can be seen off in the distance.

Waianapanapa State Park: In east Maui, a few miles before Hana, the 120 acres of this state park offer 12 cabins, a caretaker's residence, a picnic area, a shoreline hiking trail, and, best of all, a black-sand beach (it's actually small black pebbles). Swimming is generally unsafe, though, due to strong waves and rip currents. But it's a great spot for picnicking, hiking along the shore, and simply sitting and relaxing.

Hamoa Beach: This half-moon-shaped, gray-sand beach (a mix of coral and lava) in a truly tropical setting is a favorite among sunbathers, snorkelers, and body surfers in Hana. The 100-foot-wide beach is about 900 feet long and sits below 30-foot, black-lava sea cliffs. An unprotected beach open to the ocean, Hamoa is often swept by powerful rip currents. The surf breaks offshore and rolls in, making this a popular surfing and bodysurfing area. The calm left side is best for snorkeling in the summer

The Best Golf Courses

Kaanapali Golf Resort (tel. **808/661-3691**): All golfers, from high handicappers to near pros, will love the two challenging courses here. The North Course is a true Robert Trent Jones, Sr., design: an abundance of wide bunkers; several long, stretched-out tees; and the largest, most contoured greens on Maui. The South Course is an Arthur Jack Snyder design; although shorter than the North Course, it requires more accuracy on the narrow, hilly fairways. Just like its sibling course, it has a water hazard on its final hole, so don't tally up your score card until you sink your final putt.

Kapalua Resort (tel. **877/527-2582**): Kapalua Resort has probably the best nationally known golf resort in Hawaii, due to the PGA Hyundai Tournament of Champions played here each January. The Bay Course and the Village Course are vintage Arnold Palmer designs; the Plantation Course is a strong entry from Ben Crenshaw and Bill Coore. All sit on Maui's wind-swept northwestern shore, at the rolling foothills of Puu Kukui, the summit of the West Maui Mountains.

Makena Golf Courses (tel. **808/879-3344**): Here you'll find 36 holes by "Mr. Hawaii Golf" Robert Trent Jones, Jr. at his best. Add to that spectacular views: Molokini islet looms in the background, humpback whales gambol offshore in winter, and the tropical sunsets are spectacular. The South Course has magnificent views (bring your camera) and is kinder to golfers who haven't played for a while. The North Course is more difficult but also more stunning. The 13th hole, located partway up the mountain, has a view that makes most golfers stop and stare. The next hole is even more memorable: a 200-foot drop between tee and green.

Wailea Resort (tel. **888/328-MAUI** [6284]): On the sun-baked south shore of Maui stands Wailea Resort, *the* hot spot for golf in the islands. You'll find great golf at these three resort courses: The Blue Course is an Arthur Jack Snyder design, while the Emerald and Gold courses are both by Robert Trent Jones, Jr. All boast outstanding views of the Pacific and the mid-Hawaiian Islands.

The Best Inns and Bed & Breakfasts

Old Wailuku Inn at Ulupono (tel. **800/305-4899** or 808/244-5897; www.mauiinn.com): Located in historic Wailuku, the most charming town in central Maui, this restored 1924 former plantation manager's home is the place to stay if you're looking for a night in the old Hawaii of the 1920s. The guest rooms are spacious, with exotic ohia-wood floors and traditional Hawaiian quilts. The morning meal is a full gourmet breakfast served on the enclosed back lanai or on a tray delivered to your room if you prefer. Rates start at $165.

Maui Guest House (tel. **800/621-8942** or 808/661-8085; www.mauiguesthouse.com): This is one of the great bed-and-breakfast deals in Lahaina: a charming inn offering more amenities than the expensive Kaanapali hotels just down the road. The spacious home features floor-to-ceiling windows, parquet floors, and a large swimming pool. Guest rooms have quiet lanai and romantic Jacuzzis. Breakfasts are a gourmet affair. All units are $169 double.

Nona Lani Cottages (tel. **800/733-2688** or 808/879-2497; www.nonalanicottages.com): Picture this: a grassy expanse dotted with eight cottages tucked among palm, fruit, and sweet-smelling flower trees, right across the street from a white-sand beach. This is one of the great hidden deals in Kihei. The cottages are tiny but contain everything you'll need. At $95 a night, this is a deal.

Pineapple Inn Maui (tel. **877/212-MAUI** [6284] or 808/298-4403; www.pineappleinnmaui.com): This charming inn (only four rooms, plus a darling two-bedroom cottage) is not only an exquisite find, but also a terrific value (rates start at $139 a night). Located in the residential Maui Meadows area, with panoramic ocean views, this two-story inn features a giant saltwater pool and Jacuzzi overlooking the ocean. Each of the soundproof rooms is expertly decorated with a small kitchenette, comfy bed, free wireless Internet access, TV/VCR, and an incredible view off your own private lanai.

Two Mermaids on Maui B&B (tel. **800/598-9550** or 808/874-8687; www.twomermaids.com): Two avid scuba divers are the hosts at this very friendly Kihei B&B, professionally decorated in brilliant, tropical colors, complete with hand-painted art of the island (above and below the water) in a quiet neighborhood just a short 10-minute walk from the beach. Comfy rooms start at $115, including breakfast.

What a Wonderful World B&B (tel. **800/943-5804** or 808/879-9103; www.amauibedandbreakfast.com): Another one of Kihei's best B&Bs offers a great central location in town just 1/2 mile to Kamaole II Beach Park, 5 minutes from Wailea golf courses, and convenient to shopping and restaurants. All rooms boast cooking facilities and private entrances, bathrooms, and phones. A family-style breakfast (eggs Benedict, Alaskan waffles, skillet eggs with mushroom sauce, fruit blintzes) is served on the lanai, which has views of white-sand beaches, the West Maui Mountains, and Haleakala. Double rooms start at $89.

Ekena (tel. **808/248-7047;** www.ekenamaui.com): Situated on 8 1/2 acres in the hills above Hana, this Hawaiian-style wooden pole house, with 360-degree views of the coastline, the ocean, and Hana's verdant rainforest, is perfect for those in search of a quiet, peaceful vacation. Inside, the elegantly furnished home features floor-to-ceiling sliding-glass doors and a fully equipped kitchen; outside, hiking trails into the rainforest start right on the property. Beaches, waterfalls, and pools are mere minutes away. Rates start at $225 for two.

Hamoa Bay House & Bungalow (tel. **808/248-7884**): This enchanting retreat sits on 4 verdant acres within walking distance of Hamoa Beach, just outside Hana. The romantic 600-square-foot Balinese-style cottage has a full kitchen and hot tub. This very private place is perfect for honeymooners. The price? Just $225.

www.ingramcontent.com/pod-product-compliance
Lightning Source LLC
Chambersburg PA
CBHW021054080526
44587CB00010B/243